MICROSOFT®
POWERPOINT®
2013
Instructor's Guide

M000275866

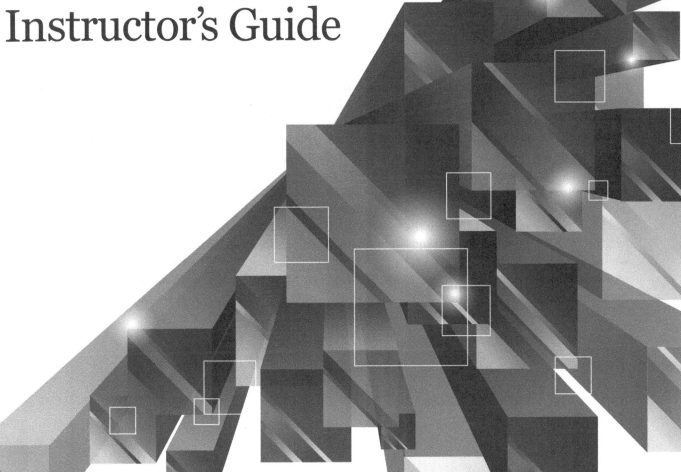

NITA RUTKOSKY
Pierce College at Puyallup
Puyallup, Washington

AUDREY ROGGENKAMP
Pierce College at Puyallup
Puyallup, Washington

IAN RUTKOSKY
Pierce College at Puyallup
Puyallup, Washington

PARADIGM
EDUCATION SOLUTIONS
St. Paul

Director of Editorial: Christine Hurney
Director of Production: Timothy W. Larson
Production Editor: Lori Michelle Ryan
Assistant Production Editor: Katherine Lee
Cover Designers: Leslie Anderson and Valerie King
Design & Production Specialist: Valerie King

Care has been taken to verify the accuracy of information presented in this book. However, the authors, editors, and publisher cannot accept responsibility for Web, email, newsgroup, or chat room subject matter or content, or for consequences from application of the information in this book, and make no warranty, expressed or implied, with respect to its content.

Trademarks: Some of the product names and company names included in this book have been used for identification purposes only and may be trademarks or registered trade names of their respective manufacturers and sellers. The authors, editors, and publisher disclaim any affiliation, association, or connection with, or sponsorship or endorsement by, such owners.

We have made every effort to trace the ownership of all copyrighted material and to secure permission from copyright holders. In the event of any question arising as to the use of any material, we will be pleased to make the necessary corrections in future printings. Thanks are due to the aforementioned authors, publishers, and agents for permission to use the materials indicated.

ISBN 978-0-76385-455-3 (Text + Disc)
ISBN 978-0-76385-384-6 (Text)

© Paradigm Publishing, Inc.
875 Montreal Way
St. Paul, MN 55102
Email: educate@emcp.com
Website: www.emcp.com

Printed in the United States of America

22 21 20 19 18 17 16 15   4 5 6 7 8 9 10

Contents

Planning the Course

Most educators would agree that the key to teaching a successful course is careful, thorough planning. And, as noted in *Exceptional Teaching: Ideas in Action*, published by Paradigm Publishing, "Instructors assess, plan, implement, and evaluate . . . repeatedly. They do this based on many of the factors that make teaching learner-centered and on several other variables. Before students even think about entering or logging into the classroom, instructors make decisions about the course. These begin with identifying the heart of the course. That is, what, exactly, are the most important outcomes that students should achieve? And what plan of action can the instructor devise that will help ensure those outcomes?" Thinking through a course action plan typically includes four phases:

1. Developing course outcomes
2. Determining the course delivery mode and structure (dividing the course into parts, each with outcomes) `
3. Selecting the instructional approach, resources, and activities of the course
4. Developing an assessment strategy

Developing Course Outcomes

In developing course outcomes, some of the key issues to consider are the following:

- When this course is complete, in what ways will the learner be permanently changed? Should instruction result in
    o building knowledge?
    o developing higher-order thinking?
    o developing independent learning skills?
    o developing technical literacy?
- What problems are encountered that are related to course content?
    o What must be communicated?
    o How will the learner find out whether the work is satisfactory?
    o How will the learner receive feedback?

Considering these questions, a set of end-of-course outcomes for a one-semester course on Microsoft PowerPoint 2013 could include the following items, stated as performance objectives.

At course conclusion, the student will be able to:

- Plan, create, and revise presentations, including executing basic skills such as opening, editing, running, saving, and closing a presentation
- Format slides using design templates, slide and title masters, styles, bullets and numbering, headers and footers, and speaker notes
- Create visual appeal with images, SmartArt, charts, animation effects, and sound and video effects
- Share presentations for collaboration and review with others
- Given a workplace scenario requiring a numbers-based solution, assess the information requirements and then prepare the materials that achieve the goal efficiently and effectively

Determining the Course Delivery Mode and Structure

Frequently, the course structure has been determined in advance by your department. However, if you are in a position to develop a plan or modify an existing structure, consider these questions:

- What topics in each subject area are essential for demonstrating the course outcomes?
- Is this the only course that will address this subject and skill set?
- What do students already know about each subject? What can they learn on their own without your direct instruction?
- Where in each subject will the instruction begin and end?

Your answers to these questions will help you divide the course content into parts and identify the associated learning outcomes (also called performance objectives). Note that course outcomes are marked by higher and more challenging skill sets and typically require the integration of many skills, while unit or part outcomes are more narrowly defined and focused.

Course Delivery: Traditional Classroom, Online (Distance Learning), or Hybrid?

While the core considerations are the same whether you are planning a traditional on-campus course, an online course (also called a distance learning course), or a hybrid of the two, the instructional delivery differences create distinct needs you must address in the planning stage.

A critical challenge in teaching online courses is the issue of interacting with students. How will you communicate with them? How will they submit assignments and tests? How will you deliver feedback? How will you get to know your students? Here are some additional questions to consider when planning an online or hybrid course:

- What course management system will you use: Blackboard or some other platform?
- Will students work independently offline? How will they use the course management system to review course outcomes, the syllabus, and assignment due dates? How will they communicate with you, take online quizzes, transmit completed work, and participate in chat sessions?
- Will you be able to offer an on-campus orientation meeting for students at the beginning of the course? If so, how will you prepare to answer the questions students will likely have?
- Will students come to the campus or school to take exams? If not, will students be directed to offsite locations where exams can be administered to verify that the person taking the exam is indeed the person getting credit for the course?
- What hardware configuration and/or software requirements must a student have to participate in your course?

Both the student and instructor resources offered with *Benchmark Microsoft PowerPoint 2013* can be adapted for use in an online learning environment or a hybrid of traditional and online learning contexts. The SNAP Training and Assessment product, in particular, is well suited for these course delivery modes, and these online files are also designed for distance-learning situations.

The Syllabus

A comprehensive syllabus will help you and your students prepare for each part of the course. A well-planned syllabus is useful for traditional, on-campus courses as well as for courses that are delivered online. A syllabus normally includes:

1. Course-identifying data
2. Prerequisites
3. Instructor contact information
4. Course outcomes
5. Required course resources
6. Major assignments
7. Grade composition
8. Class structure
9. Course schedule
10. College/school requirements

Figure 1 shows a traditional, on-campus course syllabus for a 10-week course that meets three times a week and uses *Benchmark PowerPoint 2013* as the core courseware. Lesson plans are referenced in the sample syllabus and are available on the Instructor Resources disc as well as on the password-protected part of the Internet Resource Center (IRC) for *Benchmark PowerPoint 2013* at www.ParadigmCollege.net/BenchmarkPowerPoint13. A suggestion for a 16-week semester schedule is also provided on the Instructor Resources disc and on the Internet Resource Center

FIGURE 1   Traditional 10-Week Semester Syllabus Example Using Benchmark PowerPoint 2013

Course Description
This course prepares students to work with Microsoft PowerPoint 2013 in a career setting or for personal use. Using courseware that incorporates a step-by-step, project-based approach, students develop a mastery-level competency in PowerPoint 2013 and explore the essential features of Windows 8 and Internet Explorer 10. Students also develop an understanding of fundamental computer hardware and software concepts.

Prerequisites: None

Instructor Contact Information

Name:	**Office Location:**
Office Phone:	**Office Hours:**
Office Email:	

Required Course Resources
Benchmark Series Microsoft PowerPoint 2013
        by Rutkosky, Roggenkamp, and Rutkosky © Paradigm Publishing, Inc.
Student Resources CD (provided with textbook)

Internet Resource Center, www.paradigmcollege.net/BenchmarkPowerPoint13
SNAP Training and Assessment account, snap2013.emcp.com
USB flash drive or other storage medium

Computer Time
Approximately six to eight hours per week of computer time outside of class is recommended for successful completion of course requirements.

Grading
Final grades will be calculated as an average of all of the following assignments:
- Concepts Check   5%
- Skills Check (SNAP Grade It)   10%
- Visual Benchmark   15%
- Case Study   15%
- Unit Performance Assessment   15%
- SNAP Performance Evaluations   20%
- Exams   20%

College and Course Policy Information
- This college conforms to the provisions of the Americans with Disabilities Act. You are invited to report any special needs to your instructor.
- Your attendance is expected at all class sessions.
- We subscribe to the college policy on academic honesty found in the school catalog.

Course Schedule—Benchmark Office 2013
10-week semester, three 1-hour classes per week

Week	Class	Description	Lesson Plan File or Other Resource	Chapter
1	Class 1	Getting Started, Using Windows 8, and Browsing the Internet Using Internet Explorer	BM-PowerPoint2013-Session01 BM-PowerPoint2013-Session02	Introduction 1–12; 13–39; 41–48
	Class 2	Preparing a PowerPoint Presentation	BM-PowerPoint2013-Session03 BM-PowerPoint2013-Session04	Chapter 1
	Class 3	Chapter 1 Quiz		
2	Class 4	Modifying a Presentation and Using Help	BM-PowerPoint2013-Session05	Chapter 2
	Class 5		BM-PowerPoint2013-Session06	
	Class 6	Chapter 2 Quiz		
3	Class 7	Formatting Slides	BM-PowerPoint2013-Session07	Chapter 3
	Class 8		BM-PowerPoint2013-Session08	
	Class 9	Chapter 3 Quiz		
4	Class 10	Inserting Elements in Slides	BM-PowerPoint2013-Session09	Chapter 4
	Class 11		BM-PowerPoint2013-Session10	
	Class 12	Chapter 4 Quiz		

Week	Class	Description	Lesson Plan File or Other Resource	Chapter
5	Class 13	Unit 1 Performance Assessment	BM-PowerPoint2013-Session11	Unit 1
	Class 14	Supplemental Activities	PowerPoint10-SA-L1U1 (folder)	
	Class 15	Creating Tables, Charts, and SmartArt Graphics	BM-PowerPoint2013-Session12	Chapter 5
6	Class 16	Creating Tables, Charts, and SmartArt Graphics	BM-PowerPoint2013-Session13	
	Class 17	Chapter 5 Quiz		
	Class 18	Using Slide Masters and Action Buttons	BM-PowerPoint2013-Session14	Chapter 6
7	Class 19	Using Slide Masters and Action Buttons	BM-PowerPoint2013-Session15	
	Class 20	Chapter 6 Quiz		
	Class 21	Applying Custom Animation and Setting Up Shows	BM-PowerPoint2013-Session16 BM-PowerPoint2013-Session17	Chapter 7
8	Class 22	Applying Custom Animation and Setting Up Shows	BM-PowerPoint2013-Session17 BM-PowerPoint2013-Session18	
	Class 23	Chapter 7 Quiz		
	Class 24	Integrating, Sharing, and Protecting Presentations	BM-PowerPoint2013-Session19 BM-PowerPoint2013-Session20	Chapter 8
9	Class 25	Integrating, Sharing, and Protecting Presentations	BM-PowerPoint2013-Session20 BM-PowerPoint2013-Session21	
	Class 26	Chapter 8 Quiz		
	Class 27	Supplemental Activities	PowerPoint10-SA-L1U2 (folder)	Unit 2
10	Class 28	Unit 2 Performance Assessment	BM-PowerPoint2013-Session22	
	Class 29	Theory Test	BM-PowerPoint2013-Session23	
	Class 30	Final Case Study	PowerPoint10-FinalCaseStudy-L1 (folder)	

Selecting the Instructional Approach, Resources, and Activities

After the course outcomes and structure are determined, it is important to plan the main content of the course. This includes selecting courseware, identifying resources for English language learners, considering instructional support materials, and reviewing other resources.

Student Courseware

Selecting high-quality student courseware is an important step in the planning process. Learning materials should be engaging and accessible. The Benchmark Series offers several valuable learning tools to support course performance objectives.
- *Benchmark Office 2013* textbook with Student Resources CD
- eBook
- Student Internet Resource Center at www.paradigmcollege.net/ BenchmarkOffice13

- SNAP Training and Assessment software
- SNAP Tutorials CD
- Blackboard cartridge

Textbook Structure and Features

Benchmark PowerPoint 2013 prepares students to work with *Microsoft PowerPoint 2013* in business and academic settings, and also for personal use. Incorporating a project-based approach that organizes instruction and guided exercises around related program features, this text builds student competency in the 2013 version of PowerPoint and the essential features of Windows 8 and Internet Explorer 10.

The *PowerPoint 2013* text is just one book in the *Benchmark Series. The Benchmark Series contains the following eleven textbooks*:

- *Benchmark Series Microsoft Office 2013*
  - o Getting Started (essential computer hardware and software concepts)
  - o Windows 8
  - o Internet Explorer 10
  - o Word 2013 (8 chapters)
  - o Excel 2013 (8 chapters)
  - o Access 2013 (8 chapters)
  - o PowerPoint 2013 (8 chapters)
  - o Integrating Office 2013 Programs
- *Benchmark Series Microsoft Word 2013 Levels 1 and 2*
  - o Getting Started
  - o Windows 8
  - o Internet Explorer 10
  - o Word 2013 Level 1 (8 chapters)
  - o Word 2013 Level 2 (8 chapters)
- *Benchmark Series Microsoft Word 2013 Level 1*
  - o Getting Started
  - o Windows 8
  - o Internet Explorer 10
  - o Word 2013 Level 1 (8 chapters)
- *Benchmark Series Microsoft Word 2013 Level 2*
  - o Word 2013 Level 2 (8 chapters)
- *Benchmark Series Microsoft Excel 2013 Levels 1 and 2*
  - o Getting Started
  - o Windows 8
  - o Internet Explorer 10
  - o Excel 2013 Level 1 (8 chapters)
  - o Excel 2013 Level 2 (8 chapters)
- *Benchmark Series Microsoft Excel 2013 Level 1*
  - o Getting Started
  - o Windows 8
  - o Internet Explorer 10

- o   Excel 2013 Level 1 (8 chapters)
- *Benchmark Series Microsoft Excel 2013 Level 2*
  - o   Excel 2013 Level 2 (8 chapters)
- *Benchmark Series Microsoft Access 2013 Levels 1 and 2*
  - o   Getting Started
  - o   Windows 8
  - o   Internet Explorer 10
  - o   Access 2013 Level 1 (8 chapters)
  - o   Access 2013 Level 2 (8 chapters)
- *Benchmark Series Microsoft Access 2013 Level 1*
  - o   Getting Started
  - o   Windows 8
  - o   Internet Explorer 10
  - o   Access 2013 Level 1 (8 chapters)
- *Benchmark Series Microsoft Access 2013 Level 2*
  - o   Access 2013 Level 2 (8 chapters)
- *Benchmark Series Microsoft PowerPoint 2013*
  - o   Getting Started
  - o   Windows 8
  - o   Internet Explorer 10
  - o   PowerPoint 2013 (8 chapters)

The main Microsoft application sections of each book in the Benchmark Series contain eight chapters, split into two units. The opening page of a unit lists the four chapter titles included in the unit. Each chapter opener presents the chapter's Performance Objectives, an overview of the skills taught in the chapter, a listing of the SNAP tutorials that support the chapter content, and a CD icon and text identifying a folder of data files to be copied to the student's storage medium. These files are used to complete chapter projects and end-of-chapter activities. Following the opening page, the chapter begins with model answers of the chapter projects that students can reference to confirm they have completed the chapter projects correctly.

Skills instruction in the text is organized around projects that require using a group of related features to complete a document or build a file. A project overview, which lists the project number and title, identifies tasks to accomplish and the features to use in completing the work. The project overview also identifies the number of parts that make up the project. Following each project part (identified with the project number and letter), the text presents instruction on the features and skills necessary to accomplish the next section of the project. Typically, a file remains open throughout all parts of the project. Students save their work incrementally and usually print only at the end of the entire project. Instructors have access to the live project model answer files for the completed project as well as the project parts on the Instructor Resources disc and on the password-protected Instructor section of www.paradigmcollege.net/BenchmarkOffice13.

Page margins include the following elements:
- Quick Steps—brief feature summaries for reference and review
- Hint boxes—trouble-shooting ideas and additional useful information
- Button graphics

Each chapter ends with the following review elements and exercises:
- Chapter Summary—A bulleted list captures the purpose and execution of key features.
- Commands Review—Commands taught in the chapter are listed with button, ribbon tab, and keyboard actions.
- Concepts Check—Short-answer questions allow students to test their comprehension and recall of program features, terminology, and functions. Printouts of the Concepts Check answer keys are provided in the print *Instructor's Guide* and electronic files are available on the Instructor Resources disc and on the password-protected Instructor section of www. paradigmcollege.net/BenchmarkPowerPoint13.
- Skills Check—Semi-guided exercises ask students to demonstrate their mastery of the major features and program skills taught in the chapter. The *Instructor's Guide* includes printed versions of the Skills Check model answers along with rubrics to assess student work. In addition, rubric Word documents, PDF files of the model answers, and live application model answers are available for instructors on the Instructor Resources disc and on the password-protected Instructor section of www.paradigmcollege.net/BenchmarkPowerPoint13. Items marked with a SNAP Grade It icon have corresponding SNAP activities available online.
- Visual Benchmark—With limited guidance, students are challenged to use their problem-solving skills and mastery of program features to build a file that matches a shown sample file. Grading rubrics, PDF files, and live application model answers are available to instructors to support these activities.
- Case Study—Framed in a workplace project perspective, these less-guided assessments evaluate students' abilities to apply chapter skills and concepts in solving realistic problems. Case Study activities require demonstrating program skills as well as decision-making skills and include Help and Internet-based activities. Grading rubrics, PDF files, and live application model answers are available to instructors to support these activities.

Unit Performance Assessments follow each set of four chapters and offer opportunities for cross-disciplinary, comprehensive evaluation. There are four types of Unit Performance Assessments. Assessing Proficiency is a group of gently guided exercises. Writing Activities involve applying program skills in a communication context. An Internet Research project reinforces research, writing, and program skills. A Job Study activity in the Unit 2 Performance Assessment presents a capstone assessment requiring critical thinking and problem solving. Annotated printouts of the model answers and rubrics for evaluating student work are included in the *Instructor's Guide*. The Instructor Resources disc and the password-protected Instructor section of www.paradigmcollege. net/BenchmarkPowerPoint13 include live file model answers and rubric Word document files for these assessments.

Student Resources CD

Files that serve as a starting point for completing many of the project and end-of-chapter exercises are included on the CD that accompanies the student text. Typically, students are directed to open one of these files, save the file with a new name, and then edit and print the file. Some chapter work requires the students to start an activity from a blank file. As students begin a chapter, they should copy the folder of files for the chapter exercises to the storage medium of their choice. This folder name is displayed next to a CD icon on the first page of the chapter.

eBook

For student who prefer studying with an eBook, the texts in the Benchmark Series are available in an electronic form. The web-based, password-protected eBooks feature dynamic navigation tools, including bookmarking, a linked table of contents, and the ability to jump to a specific page. The eBook format also supports helpful study tools, such as highlighting and note taking.

Benchmark PowerPoint 2013 Internet Resource Center

The Benchmark PowerPoint 2013 Resource Center at www.paradigmcollege.net/ BenchmarkPowerPoint13 offers valuable information for both instructors and students. For students, the Internet Resource Center includes quick access to the student data files, informational Web links, study aids such as online quizzes, and more. All instructor resources posted on the website are password protected and are not accessible by students.

SNAP Training and Assessment

SNAP is a web-based training and assessment program designed to optimize skill-based learning for PowerPoint along with Windows and Internet Explorer. SNAP creates a virtual classroom on the Web, allowing instructors to employ an electronic grade book and schedule tutorials, skill and concept exams, Grade It end-of-chapter Skills Check activities, and comprehensive performance evaluations.

SNAP contains:

- a bank of 79 interactive, gradable, multimedia tutorials, aligned to textbook chapters, that can be used for direct instruction or remediation (See Table 1 for a listing of the SNAP tutorials that are available for Benchmark PowerPoint 2013.)
- a bank of 144 performance skill items in which students perform tasks in Microsoft PowerPoint 2013 that are evaluated and reported in the learning management system; instructors can assign pre-defined skills exams or create their own exam from the item bank
- a bank of 20 Grade It Skills Assessment activities, which correspond to end-of-chapter activities
- comprehensive Performance Evaluation activities, one per chapter and one per unit for comprehensive evaluation of skills mastery
- a bank of 475 concept items that can be used to monitor student understanding of computer literacy and technical knowledge; instructors can assign pre-defined concepts exams or create their own

TABLE 1 Benchmark SNAP Tutorials Correlation

Benchmark Windows 8 SNAP Tutorials

Tutorial	Tutorial Title
1	Exploring the Windows 8 Start Screen
2	Exploring the Windows 8 Desktop
3	Opening and Using Windows
4	Exploring the Taskbar and the Charm Bar
5	Browsing Devices and Files
6	Selecting, Copying, and Moving Folders and Files
7	Changing Folder and View Options
8	Creating a Folder and Renaming a Folder or File
9	Using the Recycle Bin
10	Customizing the Desktop
11	Exploring the Control Panel
12	Getting Help in Windows 8
13	Using Windows Search Tools

Benchmark Internet Explorer SNAP Tutorials

Tutorial	Tutorial Title
1	Navigating the Internet Using Web Addresses
2	Finding Information Using Search Tools
3	Researching Information Using Advanced Search Tools
4	Downloading Content from a Web Page

Benchmark PowerPoint SNAP Tutorials

Chapter	Tutorial	Tutorial Title
1	1.1	Opening, Running, and Closing a Presentation
1	1.2	Creating and Saving a Presentation
1	1.3	Navigating and Inserting Slides in a Presentation
1	1.4	Changing Views and Slide Layout
1	1.5	Previewing Slides and Printing a Presentation
1	1.6	Running a Presentation
1	1.7	Adding Transition and Sound
2	2.1	Using the Spelling and Thesaurus Feature
2	2.2	Modifying Placeholders
2	2.3	Finding and Replacing Text
2	2.4	Cutting, Copying, Pasting, and Aligning Text
2	2.5	Rearranging, Deleting, and Hiding Slides
2	2.6	Duplicating and Reusing Slides
2	2.7	Creating Sections within a Presentation
2	2.8	Customizing the Quick Access Toolbar
2	2.9	Using Help in PowerPoint
3	3.1	Applying Formatting Using the Font Group
3	3.2	Applying Formatting Using the Font Dialog Box
3	3.3	Formatting with Format Painter
3	3.4	Changing Paragraph Formatting
3	3.5	Customizing Bullets and Numbering
3	3.6	Customizing Placeholders
3	3.7	Changing Page Setup

Benchmark PowerPoint SNAP Tutorials

SNAP Tutorials CD

A CD of tutorials teaching PowerPoint, Windows, and Internet Explorer skills is also available if instructors wish to assign SNAP tutorial work without using the web-based SNAP program.

Blackboard Cartridge

This set of files allows instructors to create a personalized website for their course and provides course content, tests, and the mechanisms for establishing communication via e-discussions and online group conferences. Available content includes a syllabus, test banks, PowerPoint presentations with lecture notes, and supplementary course materials. Upon request, the files can be available within 24–48 hours. Hosting the site is the responsibility of the educational institution.

Resources for English Language Learners[1]

One of the fastest growing groups of students in higher education is comprised of students whose first language is not English and whose English is not yet equivalent to that of native English speakers in lexicon and syntax. The wide differences in fluency among limited English speakers makes planning for meeting their needs somewhat more complex—and very important.

Many instructors find that they must meet the needs of students who are learning English and who need additional help. Because your goal is to help *all* the students in your course meet the intended outcomes, plan how you're going to assist students with limited English skills.

Begin by assessing the language abilities of your students:

1. One method is a "one-minute preview." Provide sheets of paper and ask students two questions. Give them one minute or so to write their answers. The questions could be about their language skills, but it might be better to ask about something else. That way you get a short writing sample plus information about something, such as why they are taking the course, what they would like to learn, the types of activities they enjoy, or what they are most worried about in the course. You will be able to see which students will need additional help.

2. If your class is small, conduct a discussion early in the course. Make sure you hear each student answer a question or ask one.

3. If you are conducting a pretest for the course, include some questions that ask students if they need to improve their English or writing skills.

4. Tell students to email you if they think they will need language help or extra exam time for reading assignments or tests.

In addition to the suggestions above, consider preparing a list of terms for each session that might be difficult for English language learners. You can suggest that students arrange for tutors to assist them with completing the unguided assessments. You may also want to dedicate a session (or part of one) to instruction on how to prepare the work you expect.

Instructor Resources

Along with the *Instructor's Guide*, instructional materials available with *Benchmark PowerPoint 2013* include:

- Instructor Resources disc with electronic files for all resources included in the *Instructor's Guide*. The disc also offers the model answer files for end-of-chapter work in live program format and annotated PDF format, PowerPoint presentations with lecture notes, and detailed lesson plans, which include lecture/demonstration

---

[1] Excerpted from *Exceptional Teaching: Ideas in Action*, published by Paradigm Publishing, Inc.

notes, discussion topics, tips for students, and possible work for advanced students.
* Instructor resources available at the Internet Resource Center at www.paradigmcollege.net/BenchmarkPowerPoint13, which includes all of the materials in the print *Instructor's Guide* and on the Instructor Resources disc.
* ExamView® Assessment Suite and test banks with approximately 475 multiple-choice items to create customized web-based or print tests.

Information about Microsoft Office 2013

Microsoft Office 2013 operates on the Windows 8 operating system, as well as on Windows 7.

Video on the What's New in Office 2013

Microsoft Corporation offers its own downloadable video presentation on the new features in Office 2013 at this address: http://office.microsoft.com/en-us/support/video-whats-new-in-office-2013-VA103147615.aspx?CTT=1http

Quick Start Guides

Microsoft provides a series of Quick Start Guides for the applications in Office 2013 at http://office.microsoft.com/en-us/support/office-2013-quick-start-guides-HA103673669.aspx?CTT=1

Certification: Microsoft Office Specialist

With the release of Office 2013, Microsoft has developed a new set of certification objectives, which are available at http://www.microsoft.com/learning/en/us/mos-certification.aspx. The following books in the Benchmark Series have been validated and approved by ProCert Labs (www.procert.com) as courseware covering the Core-level objectives in the Microsoft Office Specialist Certification exam.
* *Benchmark Series Microsoft Word 2013 Levels 1 & 2*
* *Benchmark Series Microsoft Excel 2013 Levels 1 & 2*
* *Benchmark Series Microsoft Access 2013 Levels 1 & 2*
* *Benchmark Series Microsoft PowerPoint 2013*

Table 2 correlates the *Benchmark PowerPoint 2013* text with the certification exam objectives.

TABLE 2 Benchmark PowerPoint and Microsoft Office Specialist Certification Exam Objectives Correlation

Certification Exam Objective	Text Reference
1.0 Create and Manage Presentations	
1.1 Create a Presentation	
1.1.1 create blank presentations	C1, pgs. 11-15
1.1.2 create presentations use templates	C1, pgs. 10-15; C6, pgs. 250-251; C8, pgs. 346-348
1.1.3 import text files into presentations	C8, pgs. 329-331; 342-346

Certification Exam Objective	Text Reference
1.14 import Word document outlines into presentations	C8, pgs. 328-329
1.2 Format a Presentation Using Slide Masters	
1.2.1 apply a slide master	C6, pgs. 237-240
1.2.2 add new layouts	C6, pgs. 239-242; 244-246
1.2.3 modify existing layouts	C6, pgs. 244-246
1.2.4 add background images	C6, pgs. 240-241
1.2.5 control page numbers	C6, pgs. 247, 249
1.2.6 insert headers and footers	C6, pgs. 243-244
1.2.7 modify presentation themes	C6, pgs. 238-239; 247, 249
1.3 Customize Presentation Options and Views	
1.3.1 change page setup options	C3, pgs. 103-104
1.3.2 change to view in color/grayscale	C6, pgs. 256-257
1.3.3 demonstrate how to use views to navigate through presentations	C1, pgs.16-18
1.3.4 modify presentation properties	C8, pgs. 353-355
1.4 Configure Presentations to Print or Save	
1.4.1 set handout print options	C1, pgs. 18-22
1.4.2 print selections from presentations	C1, pgs. 18-22; C2, pgs. 63-65
1.4.3 package presentations for CD	C8, pgs. 335-336
1.4.4 save presentations as web pages	C7, pgs. 304-305 (presenting a presentation online); C8, pgs. 334-336 (exporting presentations, saving a presentation as a video)
1.4.5 print presentations in grayscale	C6, pgs. 256-257
1.4.6 print speaker notes	C1, pgs. 18-22
1.4.7 maintain backward compatibility	C8, pgs. 362-365
1.5 Configure and Present Slideshows	
1.5.1 create custom slideshows	C7, pgs. 306-308
1.5.2 configure slideshow options	C1, pgs. 22-26
1.5.3 rehearse timing	C7, pgs. 299-300
1.5.4 configure slideshow resolution	C1, pgs. 103-104
1.5.5 demonstrate how to use Presenter View	C7, pgs. 303-304
1.5.6 navigate within slideshows	C1, pgs. 8-9, 16-18
1.5.7 annotate slideshows	C1, pgs. 22-26
2.0 Insert and Format Shapes and Slides	
2.1 Insert and Format Slides	
2.1.1 add slides layouts	C1, pgs. 11-15
2.1.2 duplicate existing slides	C2, pgs. 60-61
2.1.3 hide slides	C7, pgs. 302-304
2.1.4 delete slides	C2, pgs. 48-49, 57-58
2.1.5 modify slide backgrounds	C3, pgs. 105-108

Certification Exam Objective	Text Reference
2.1.6 apply styles to slides	C3, pgs. 98-103; C2, pgs. 105-108
2.2 Insert and Format Shapes	
2.2.1 modify shape backgrounds	C4, pgs. 138, 141
2.2.2 apply borders to shapes	C4, pgs. 138, 142
2.2.3 resize shapes	C4, pg. 139
2.2.4 insert shapes	C4, pgs. 135, 138
2.2.5 create custom shapes	C4, pgs. 140-141
2.2.6 apply styles to shapes	C4, pgs. 138, 142
2.3 Order and Group Shapes and Slides	
2.3.1 insert section headers	C2, pgs. 63-65
2.3.2 modify slide order	C2, pgs. 57-58
2.3.3 align and group shapes	C4, pgs. 130, 141-142
2.3.4 display gridlines	C4, pgs. 136-139
3.0 Create Slide Content	
3.1 Insert and Format Text	
3.1.1 change text to WordArt	C4, pgs. 154-156
3.1.2 create multiple columns in a single shape	C3, pgs. 87, 90-92; C4, pgs. 127, 129
3.1.3 insert hyperlinks	C6, pgs. 262-266
3.1.4 apply formatting and styles to text	C3, pgs. 81-89
3.1.5 create bulleted and numbered lists	C1, pgs. 14, 17, 29-30; C3, pgs. 94-98
3.2 Insert and Format Tables	
3.2.1 create new tables	C5, pgs. 189-198
3.2.2 modify number of rows and columns	C5, pgs. 193
3.2.3 apply table styles	C5, pgs. 191-192
3.2.4 import tables from external sources	C5, pgs. 195-197
3.3 Insert and Format Charts	
3.3.1 create and modify chart styles	C5, pgs. 206-217
3.3.2 insert charts	C5, pgs. 208
3.3.3 modify chart type	C5, pgs. 210-211
3.3.4 add legends to charts	C5, pgs. 208-209; 213-214
3.3.5 modify chart parameters	C5, pg. 209-210
3.3.6 import charts from external sources	C8, pgs. 342-346
3.4 Insert and Format SmartArt	
3.4.1 add shapes to SmartArt	C5, pg. 203
3.4.2 change color of SmartArt	C5, pgs. 200, 202, 204
3.4.3 move text within SmartArt shapes	C5, pgs. 203-205
3.4.4 reverse directions	C5, pg. 204
3.4.5 convert lists to SmartArt	C5, pgs. 203-205
3.5 Insert and Format Images	
3.5.1 resize images	C4, pgs. 143-145
3.5.2 crop images	C4, pgs. 143-145

Certification Exam Objective	Text Reference
3.5.3 apply effects	C4, pgs. 142, 145-146
3.5.4 apply styles	C4, pgs. 142, 146
3.6 Insert and Format Media	
3.6.1 adjust media window size	C7, pg. 311
3.6.2 trim timing on media clips	C7, pg. 313
3.6.3 set start/stop times	C7, pgs. 309, 313
3.6.4 set media options	C7, pgs. 309-312, 314
3.6.5 link to external media	C7, pgs. 310, 312
4.0 Apply Transitions and Animations	
4.1 Apply Transitioning between Slides	
4.1.1 insert transitions between slides	C1, pgs. 31-34
4.1.2 manage multiple transitions	C1, pgs. 31-34
4.1.3 modify transition effect options	C1, pgs. 31-34
4.2 Animate Slide Content	
4.2.1 apply animations to shapes	C7, pgs. 289-290
4.2.2 apply animations to text strings	C7, pgs. 288, 292
4.2.3 add paths to animations	C7, pgs. 293-294
4.2.4 modify animation options	C7, pgs. 283-287
4.3 Set Timing for Transitions and Animations	
4.3.1 modify durations of effects	C1, pgs. 32-34; C7, pgs. 283-286
4.3.2 configure start and finish options	C7, pgs. 283-285
4.3.3 reorder animations	C7, pgs. 285-287
4.3.4 demonstrate how to use the Animation Pane	C7, pgs. 285-287
5.0 Manage Multiple Presentations	
5.1 Merge Content from Multiple Presentations	
5.1.1 merge multiple presentations	C8, pgs. 349-350
5.1.2 reuse slides from other presentations	C2, pgs. 61-63
5.1.3 view multiple presentations	C6, pgs. 255-257
5.2 Track Changes and Resolve Differences	
5.2.1 set track changes	(no track changes)
5.2.2 modify options for track changes	(no track changes)
5.2.3 discard changes from specific users	(no track changes)
5.2.4 manage comments	C8, pgs. 351-353
5.3 Protect and Share Presentations	
5.3.1 encrypt presentations with a password	C8, pgs. 355-357
5.3.2 proof presentations	C2, pgs. 45-48
5.3.3 mark as final	C8, pgs. 335-357
5.3.4 compress media	C7, pgs. 310, 312
5.3.5 embed fonts	C8, pgs. 335-336
5.3.6 restrict permissions	C8, pgs. 355, 357 (theory)
5.3.7 remove presentation metadata	C8, pgs. 350-360

Certification Exam Objective	Text Reference
5.3.8 check for accessibility issues	C8, pgs. 360-361
5.3.9 check for compatibility issues	C8, pgs. 362-363

Microsoft Office 2013 Product Editions

Microsoft Office 2013 is available in the following editions:
- Microsoft Office Starter
- Office Home and Student
- Office Home and Business
- Office Professional
- Microsoft Office Professional Plus
- Microsoft Office Standard
- Microsoft Office Professional Academic

The programs included in each edition at http://office.microsoft.com/en-us/products/FX101635841033.aspx.

Microsoft Office 2013 System Requirements

This interactive text is designed for the student to complete chapter work on a computer running a standard installation of Microsoft Office 2013, Office Professional Edition, and the Microsoft Windows 8 operating system. To effectively run the Microsoft Office 2013 suite and operating system, your computer should be outfitted with the following:
- 1 gigahertz (GHz) processor or higher; 1 gigabyte (GB) of RAM
- 3 GB of available hard-disk space
- .NET version 3.5, 4.0, or 4.5
- DirectX 10 graphics card
- Minimum 1024 × 576 monitor resolution (or 1366 × 768 to use the Windows Snap feature)
- Computer mouse, multi-touch device, or compatible pointing device

Office 2013 will also operate on computers running the Windows XP Service Pack 3 or the Windows Vista operating system.

Screen captures for the books in the Benchmark Series were created using a screen resolution display setting of 1600 × 900. Refer to the *Customizing Settings* section of *Getting Started in Office 2013,* which follows the textbook's preface for instructions on changing a monitor's resolution. Figure G.10 on page 10 of the textbook illustrates the Microsoft Office Word ribbon at three resolutions for comparison purposes. Choose the resolution that best matches your computer; however, be aware that using a resolution other than 1600 × 900 means that your screens may not match the illustrations in this book.

Developing an Assessment Strategy

The final major phase of planning a course is to develop an assessment strategy based on the purpose of evaluation and on your philosophy of what constitutes high-quality assessments. The obvious purpose of assessing students' learning is to determine whether students have achieved the goals of the course and, if they have, to what degree, resulting in a grade for credits earned. Other functions of evaluation include motivating students, determining the overall effectiveness of your teaching, and meeting accreditation requirements.

In developing your philosophy of assessment, consider these suggestions from Paradigm Publishing's *Exceptional Teaching*.

Assessments should:

- contribute to students' learning by asking them to apply their skills in out-of-school or workplace situations.
- be planned as an integral part of the course design in terms of timing, content, and form.
- have a clear purpose.
- be appropriate for the purpose in terms of content and format.
- be scored as consistently and objectively as possible.
- provide students with feedback on their learning.
- emphasize intellectual traits of value—analytical reading, thinking, decision making, and research skills along with individual creativity and intelligence.
- be conducted at specific, planned checkpoints.
- be conducted in a positive learning environment, with every effort made to lower students' test anxieties.
- allow students to demonstrate their accomplishment of outcomes in various ways, including ways that fit their individual learning styles.

Determining the Number, Level, and Type of Assessments

Formulate your evaluation and grading strategy by answering these course-level questions. Consider if you should include:

- a course pre-assessment?
- a course comprehensive assessment that will determine students' mastery of the major intended outcomes for the entire course?
- pre-assessments for each section?
- comprehensive assessments for each section that assess students' mastery of the major intended outcomes for that section?
- interim or checkpoint assessments that assess students' mastery of intended outcomes of learning within units? How many? How often?

Also ask yourself: once my system is in place, will my students know that I value *how* and *how well* they think?

These questions will help you establish approximately how many assessments you wish to include and their place in the course.

The next decisions concern which types of assessment to use: traditional cognitive (objective) tests and/or performance-based assessments. Each of these two major categories of tests has its merits. Traditional cognitive tests such as multiple-choice exams usually work best for testing information recall, comprehension, and analysis. They also are reliable and efficient, and relatively easy to score. On the down side, objective-type tests are criticized for not representing how students will use their new skills in an unfamiliar setting or in the real world of work. On the other hand, performance-based testing requires students to demonstrate what they have learned and to apply it in a realistic context that closely approximates an on-the-job situation. These tests measure how well students can do what the course intended to teach them. As emphasized in *Exceptional Teaching,* "Authentic, performance-based assessments ask students to integrate what they have learned and apply it to resolve an issue, solve a problem, create something new, work collaboratively, or use their written and oral communication skills. Authentic assessments stress the process of learning as well as the outcomes of learning."

Creating a Grading Plan

By choosing the types of assessments that will measure students' achievement of course and program outcomes, you will already have established a schema of the major grading components. The next step is to weight the scores before entering them into a grade calculation system, such as, an Excel spreadsheet.

Will you include other factors such as effort and attendance in students' grades? If so, consider how to measure those elements. While it is simple to track attendance, it is not as easy to objectively evaluate effort and attitude. Some experts recommend that teachers provide regular verbal and written feedback on these factors, but confine grades to academic achievement.

The following grading plan, which is part of the sample syllabus presented earlier in this section, offers a starting point as you develop your comprehensive grading strategy:

- Concepts Check assignments   5%
- Skills Check (SNAP Grade It) assignments   10%
- Visual Benchmark assignments   15%
- Case Study assignments   15%
- SNAP Performance Evaluations   20%
- Unit Performance Assessments   15%
- Exams   20%

For More Information

Much of the content of this "Planning the Course" article is based on information found in *Exceptional Teaching: Ideas in Action*. To order a copy of this resource, please visit www.ParadigmCollege.com or contact Customer Care at 800-535-6865, or educate@emcp.com.

Overview
Using Windows 8

Performance Objectives
- Use the Start screen to launch programs
- Use desktop icons and the Taskbar to launch programs and open files or folders
- Organize and manage data, including copying moving, creating, and deleting files and folders; and create a shortcut
- Explore the Control Panel and personalize the desktop
- Use the Windows Help and Support features
- Use search tools
- Customize monitor settings

Projects

Project 1   Opening Programs, Switching between Programs, and Manipulating Windows

Project 2   Changing Taskbar Properties

Project 3   Copying a File and Folder and Deleting a File

Project 4   Copying and Deleting Files

Project 5   Creating a New Folder

Project 6   Deleting Files to and Restoring Files from the Recycle Bin

Project 7   Emptying the Recycle Bin

Project 8   Creating a Shortcut

Project 9   Changing the Desktop Theme

Project 10   Customizing the Mouse

Project 11   Customizing with a Shortcut Command

Project12   Getting Help

Project 13   Searching for Programs and Files

Overview
Browsing the Internet Using Internet Explorer 10

Performance Objectives
- Navigate the Internet using URLs and hyperlinks
- Use search engines to locate information
- Download web pages and images

Projects
Project 1   Browsing the Internet Using URLs
Project 2   Navigating Using Hyperlinks
Project 3   Searching for Information by Topic
Project 4   Searching with a Metasearch Search Engine
Project 5   Narrowing a Search
Project 6   Downloading Images and Web Pages
Project 7   Opening the Saved Web Page and Image in a Word Document

Overview
PowerPoint 2013, Chapter 1
Preparing a PowerPoint Presentation

Performance Objectives

- Open, save, run, print, close, and delete a presentation
- Pin a presentation to a recent list
- Plan a presentation
- Create a presentation using a theme template
- Insert slides, insert text in slides, and choose slide layouts
- Change presentation views
- Navigate and edit slides
- Preview and print a presentation
- Apply a design theme and variant to a presentation
- Prepare a presentation from a blank presentation
- Prepare a presentation in Outline view
- Add transitions, sounds, and timings to a presentation

Projects

Project 1	Open and Run a Presentation
1	Opening, Running, and Closing a Presentation
Project 2	Create an Internet Presentation Using a Theme Template
2a	Creating a Presentation Using a Design Theme Template
2b	Navigating and Editing Slides in a Presentation
2c	Printing a Presentation
Project 3	Opening and Running a Presentation and Changing the Presentation Design Theme
3a	Opening and Running a Presentation
3b	Applying a Design Theme and Variant
3c	Deleting a PowerPoint Presentation
Project 4	Create a Technology Presentation in the Outline Pane
4a	Preparing a Presentation in Outline View
4b	Adding Transitions and Sounds to a Presentation
4c	Advancing Slides Automatically

Overview
PowerPoint 2013, Chapter 2
Modifying a Presentation and Using Help

Performance Objectives

- Check spelling
- Use the Thesaurus
- Insert and delete text in slides
- Find and replace text in slides
- Cut, copy, and paste text in slides
- Rearrange text in the slide thumbnails pane
- Size and rearrange placeholders
- Insert, delete, move, and copy slides
- Copy slides between presentations
- Duplicate slides
- Reuse slides
- Create and manage sections
- Customize the Quick Access toolbar
- Use the Help feature

Projects

Project 1   Check Spelling, Use the Thesaurus, and Manage Text in a Design Presentation
    1a   Checking the Spelling in a Presentation
    1b   Inserting and Deleting Text in Slides
    1c   Finding and Replacing Text
Project 2   Cut, Copy, Paste, Rearrange, and Manage Slides in a Network Presentation
    2a   Cutting, Copying, and Pasting Text in Slides
    2b   Rearranging Text in the Slide Thumbnails Pane
    2c   Sizing and Rearranging Placeholders
    2d   Moving and Copying Slides
    2e   Copying Slides between Presentations
Project 3   Insert and Manage Slides in an Adventure Tours Presentation
    3a   Duplicating Selected Slides
    3b   Reusing Slides
    3c   Creating and Printing Sections
    3d   Customizing the Quick Access Toolbar
Project 4   Use PowerPoint Help Feature and Create a Presentation
    4   Using the Help Feature and Creating a Presentation

Overview
PowerPoint 2013, Chapter 3
Formatting Slides

Performance Objectives
- Apply font and paragraph formatting to text in slides
- Apply formatting with the Mini toolbar and Format Painter
- Customize bullets and numbers
- Change page setup
- Customize slide backgrounds
- Create custom themes including custom theme colors and theme fonts
- Delete custom themes

Projects

Project 1 Format an E-Commerce Presentation
    1a Applying Font Formatting to Text
    1b Applying Formatting with Format Painter
    1c Applying Paragraph Formatting to Text
    1d Customizing Paragraph and Column Formatting
    1e Rotating and Vertically Aligning Text
Project 2 Customize Bullets and Numbers and Change Page Setup in a Color Presentation
    2a Customizing Bullets and Numbers
    2b Customizing Numbers
    2c Customizing Placeholders
    2d Changing Orientation and Page Setup
Project 3 Modify the Theme and Slide Background of a Network Presentation
    3 Customizing Theme Colors, Theme Fonts, and Slide Background
Project 4 Create and Apply Custom Themes to Presentations
    4a Creating Custom Theme Colors
    4b Creating Custom Theme Fonts
    4c Saving and Applying a Custom Theme
    4d Deleting Custom Themes

Overview
PowerPoint 2013, Chapter 4
Inserting Elements in Slides

Performance Objectives

- Insert, format, select, and align a text box
- Set tabs in a text box
- Insert, format, and copy shapes
- Display rulers, gridlines, and guides
- Group and ungroup objects
- Insert, crop, size, move, and format a picture
- Insert a picture as a slide background
- Insert, size, scale, rotate, and position a clip art image
- Create and insert a screenshot
- Create and format WordArt text
- Insert objects such as a header, footer, date, slide number, and symbol

Projects

Project 1	Create a Company Presentation Containing Text Boxes, Shapes, and Images
1a	Inserting and Formatting Text Boxes
1b	Formatting a Text Box and Setting the Default Text Box
1c	Creating a Text Box and Setting Tabs
1d	Drawing and Formatting Shapes
1e	Merging Shapes
1f	Grouping and Formatting Objects
1g	Inserting and Formatting Pictures
1h	Inserting a Picture as a Slide Background
1i	Inserting and Formatting a Clip Art Image
1j	Copying an Object within and between Presentations
1k	Inserting and Formatting a Screenshot
1l	Inserting and Formatting WordArt
1m	Inserting Symbols in a Presentation
1n	Inserting Headers and Footers

Overview
PowerPoint 2013, Chapter 5
Creating Tables, Charts, and SmartArt Graphics

Performance Objectives
- Create and format a table
- Modify the design and layout of a table
- Insert an image in a table
- Create SmartArt graphics
- Modify the design and layout of SmartArt
- Convert text to a SmartArt graphic
- Create and format charts
- Modify the design and layout of charts
- Select and format chart elements
- Create, edit, and format a photo album

Projects

Project 1	Create a Company Sales Conference Presentation
1a	Creating a Table
1b	Modifying the Table Design
1c	Modifying the Table Layout
1d	Inserting and Formatting an Excel Spreadsheet in a Slide
1e	Drawing a Table
1f	Inserting and Modifying a SmartArt Graphic
1g	Inserting and Formatting a SmartArt Graphic
1h	Creating a SmartArt Graphic with Text and WordArt
1i	Converting SmartArt to Text and to Shapes
1j	Creating a Chart
1k	Creating a Chart
1l	Changing the Chart Design
1m	Formatting a Chart and Chart Elements
1n	Creating and Formatting a Pie Chart
Project 2	Create and Format a Travel Photo Album
2a	Creating a Travel Photo Album
2b	Editing and Formatting a Photo Album
2c	Formatting Pictures in a Presentation

Overview
PowerPoint 2013, Chapter 6
Using Slide Masters and Action Buttons

Performance Objectives
- Format slides in Slide Master view
- Apply themes and backgrounds in Slide Master view
- Delete placeholders and slide master layouts
- Insert elements in Slide Master view
- Create and rename a custom slide layout
- Insert a new slide master
- Save a presentation as a template
- Customize a handout in Handout Master view
- Customize notes pages in Notes Master view
- Change zoom, manage windows, and view presentations in color and grayscale
- Insert action buttons
- Insert hyperlinks

Projects

Project 1		Create a Travel Presentation and Apply Formatting in Slide Master View
	1a	Formatting a Slide Master
	1b	Applying and Formatting Background Graphics
	1c	Inserting Slides in a Presentation
	1d	Inserting Elements in Slide Master View
	1e	Inserting a Layout and Placeholder
	1f	Applying a Second Slide Master
Project 2		Save a Template and Create a Travel Presentation with the Template
	2a	Saving a Presentation as a Template
	2b	Customizing the Handout Master
	2c	Customizing the Notes Master
	2d	Viewing a Presentation
Project 3		Insert Action Buttons and Hyperlinks in a Job Search Presentation
	3a	Inserting Action Buttons
	3b	Linking to Another Presentation and a Website
	3c	Inserting Hyperlinks to a Website
	3d	Inserting Hyperlinks to a Website, to Another Presentation, and to a Word Document
	3e	Modifying, Editing, and Removing a Hyperlink

Overview
PowerPoint 2013, Chapter 7
Applying Custom Animation and Setting Up Shows

Performance Objectives
- Apply animations
- Modify and remove animations
- Apply a build
- Animate shapes, images, SmartArt, and chart elements
- Draw motion paths
- Set up a slide show
- Set rehearse timings for slides
- Hide slides
- Create, run, edit, and print a custom show
- Insert and customize audio and video files

Projects

Project 1	Apply Animation Effects to Elements in a Marketing Presentation
1a	Applying Animations
1b	Removing Animations
1c	Applying Animation Effects
1d	Removing, Modifying, and Reordering Animation Effects
1e	Removing, Modifying, and Reordering Animation Effects in the Animation Pane
1f	Applying Sound and a Build to Animations
Project 2	Apply Custom Animation Effects to Elements in Slides in an Online Learning Presentation
2a	Animating Shapes and a Clip Art Image
2b	Animating SmartArt
2c	Animating Elements in a Chart
2d	Drawing a Motion Path
2e	Inserting Triggers
2f	Running a Presentation without Animation
Project 3	Prepare a Self-Running Adventure Presentation and Create Custom Shows
3a	Preparing a Self-Running Presentation
3b	Setting Rehearse Timings for Slides
3c	Optional: Recording Narration
3d	Hiding Slides and Using Presenter View
3e	Optional: Presenting Online
3f	Creating, Editing, and Running Custom Shows

Overview
PowerPoint 2013, Chapter 8
Integrating, Sharing, and Protecting Presentations

Performance Objectives

- Import a Word outline into a presentation
- Copy and paste data between programs and use the Clipboard
- Share presentations with others
- Export a presentation to Word
- Save a presentation in different file formats
- Embed and link objects
- Download templates
- Compare and combine presentations
- Insert, edit, and delete comments
- Manage presentation properties
- Protect a presentation
- Inspect a presentation and check for accessibility and compatibility issues
- Manage versions of presentations
- Customize PowerPoint options

Projects

Overview of Assessment Venues

The grading sheet on the following pages can be used as a resource to create your grading plan. An electronic copy of this table is provided on the Instructor Resources disc, and you can alter this file to meet your specific course needs. Several venues of different types are available for assessing student achievement in your course.

Comprehension-Based Assessments

- Concepts Check questions appear at the end of each chapter. These short-answer questions test student comprehension and recall of program features, terminology, and functions. Answer keys are included in the *Instructor's Guide*, on the Instructor Resources disc, and on the password-protected Instructor section of the Internet Resource Center. Matching activities based on the Concepts Check questions are available in SNAP.
- ExamView® test generating software and test banks includes multiple-choice items for each chapter of the text. Use ExamView to create web-based or print tests.
- SNAP web-based assessments include multiple-choice items for each chapter of the text (prepared from the ExamView test banks). Instructors can assign pre-designed concepts exams or create their own.
- Quizzes of multiple-choice items for each chapter of the text (different from the items in the ExamView test banks) are available on the Internet Resource Center. Students can take quizzes in either practice mode with immediate feedback or in scores-reported mode with results emailed to the instructor.

Performance-Based Assessments

- End-of-chapter assessments are provided to assess student understanding of major features and program skills taught in the chapter. Instructor support for these assessments is included in the *Instructor's Guide*, on the Instructor Resources disc and, on the password-protected Instructor section of the Internet Resource Center.
  - o Skills Check assessments provide additional hands-on computer exercises to reinforce learning. These exercises include some guidance, but less than the chapter projects. Items marked with a SNAP Grade It icon have a corresponding activity available in SNAP, which will automatically score student work. Grading rubrics, annotated PDF files, and live application files are available to instructors to support these activities.
  - o Visual Benchmark activities provide limited guidance and challenge students to use their problem-solving skills and mastery of program features to build a file that matches a file displayed with the exercise. Grading rubrics, PDF files, and live application files are available to instructors to support these activities.
  - o Case Studies offer realistic scenarios that require taking initiative and determining solutions using skills developed throughout the chapter. Students search the Internet or the program's Help feature to find the additional information they need to create final documents and files. Student work will vary, but grading rubrics, PDF files, and live application files are available to instructors to support these activities.

- Unit Performance Assessments are separate sections at the end of each group of four chapters that include a range of activities to evaluate student achievement. Grading rubrics are provided to instructors to support these activities.
  o Assessing Proficiency exercises involve using program features to create a variety of documents, all with little or no assistance. Annotated PDF files and live application files are available to instructors to support these activities.
  o Writing Activities stress the vital cross-disciplinary skill of writing clearly during the course of preparing specific documents.
  o Internet Research is a scenario-based activity requiring Internet navigation and searching plus information analysis and presentation.
  o Job Study is a culminating case study exercise that simulates workplace tasks and challenges. This Performance Assessment type is found in Unit 2 Performance Assessments.
- SNAP is a web-based training and assessment program designed to optimize skill-based learning. SNAP includes a learning management system that creates a virtual classroom on the Web, allowing the instructor to schedule tutorials, exams, and textbook assignments and to employ an electronic grade book. SNAP support for the *Benchmark Series* includes the following:
  o A bank of 79 interactive, gradable, multimedia tutorials, aligned to support activities found in textbook sections, that can be used for direct instruction or remediation.
  o A skill item bank of 144 performance skills in which students perform tasks in Microsoft PowerPoint 2013 that are evaluated and reported in the learning management system. Instructors can assign pre-defined skill exams or create their own exams from the item bank.
  o Grade It Skills Check activities, with immediate, automatic scoring with individualized feedback of student work, align with select Skills Check activities in the textbook.
  o Comprehensive Performance Evaluation activities, one per chapter and one per unit, for comprehensive evaluation of skills mastery.
  o Over 475 concept items that can be used to monitor student understanding computer literacy and technical knowledge as well as a concept item generator that will allow instructors to create up to ten kinds of new concept items
- Supplemental activities are provided for use in evaluating student comprehension of program skills. Resources for these assessments are included in the *Instructor's Guide*, on the Instructor Resources disc, and on the Instructor section of the Internet Resource Center.
  o Supplemental Assessments are similar in format to the end-of-chapter Skills Check or Visual Benchmark assessments, and are supported with data files, model answer files, and rubrics. There is one Supplemental Assessment for each unit, or two for each level.
  o Supplemental Case Studies are similar in format to the end-of-chapter Case Studies, and are supported with, data files, model answer files, and rubrics. There is one Supplemental Case Study for each application level.

Using the Microsoft PowerPoint 2013 Compare Feature

PowerPoint 2013 includes a Compare feature that enables users to compare two different versions of a presentation. With the PowerPoint Compare feature, you can view differences between students' files and model answer files. Unlike the Word and Excel compare features, the PowerPoint Compare feature does not allow you to save or print a compare file.

Instructions for Using PowerPoint's Compare Feature

1. Close all open PowerPoint files.
2. Open the model answer file and click the REVIEW tab.
3. Click the Compare button in the Compare group to open the Choose File to Merge with Current Presentation dialog box.
4. Browse to the location where you have saved the student's file and then click the student's file to enter its name in the *File name* text box.
5. Click the Merge button to launch the Compare feature. You will now see one of two results:
   a. If the two files are identical, you will see a dialog box displaying the message "Student Name made no changes to this presentation" (with the name of the author of the student's file in place of *Student Name*).
   b. If the two files are not identical, PowerPoint shows differences between the student's file and the model answer file in comments and in the Revisions pane.
6. Unlike the Word and Excel compare features, the PowerPoint Compare feature does not allow you to save and print the compare file.

Grading Sheet

Benchmark Series Microsoft PowerPoint 2013

Assignment	Title	Start from Scratch	SNAP Grade It	Date Due	Grade
Unit 1: Creating and Formatting PowerPoint Presentations					
Chapter 1 Preparing a PowerPoint Presentation					
Concepts Check			✓		
Skills Check Assessment 1	Create a Presentation on Types of Resumes	✓	✓		
Skills Check Assessment 2	Create a Presentation on Preparing a Company Newsletter	✓	✓		
Visual Benchmark	Create a Presentation on Preparing a Newsletter	✓			
Case Study Part 1	Citizens for Consumer Safety: Smoke Detectors Presentation				
Case Study Part 2	Citizens for Consumer Safety: Smoke Detectors Presentation Printouts				
Case Study Part 3	Citizens for Consumer Safety: Online Sales (Internet)				
SNAP Tutorial 1.1	Opening, Running, and Closing a Presentation				
SNAP Tutorial 1.2	Creating and Saving a Presentation				
SNAP Tutorial 1.3	Navigating and Inserting Slides in a Presentation				
SNAP Tutorial 1.4	Changing Views and Slide Layout				
SNAP Tutorial 1.5	Previewing Slides and Printing a Presentation				
SNAP Tutorial 1.6	Running a Presentation				
SNAP Tutorial 1.7	Adding Transition and Sound				
IRC Quiz	Study Quiz				
SNAP Concepts	Quiz				
SNAP Skill Items	Quiz				
SNAP PE	Comprehensive Performance Evaluation				
Chapter 2 Modifying a Presentation and Using Help					
Concepts Check			✓		

Assignment	Title	Start from Scratch	SNAP Grade It	Date Due	Grade
Skills Check Assessment 1	Create an Electronic Design Presentation	✓	✓		
Skills Check Assessment 2	Create a Netiquette Presentation	✓	✓		
Skills Check Assessment 3	Download a Design Theme	✓			
Visual Benchmark	Formatting a Presentation on Online Learning				
Case Study Part 1	Career Finders Agency: Job Analysis				
Case Study Part 2	Career Finders Agency: Job Analysis				
Case Study Part 3	Career Finders Agency: Templates	✓			
SNAP Tutorial 2.1	Using the Spelling and Thesaurus Feature				
SNAP Tutorial 2.2	Modifying Placeholders				
SNAP Tutorial 2.3	Finding and Replacing Text				
SNAP Tutorial 2.4	Cutting, Copying, Pasting, and Aligning Text				
SNAP Tutorial 2.5	Rearranging, Deleting, and Hiding Slides				
SNAP Tutorial 2.6	Duplicating and Reusing Slides				
SNAP Tutorial 2.7	Creating Sections within a Presentation				
SNAP Tutorial 2.8	Customizing the Quick Access Toolbar				
SNAP Tutorial 2.9	Using Help in PowerPoint				
IRC Quiz	Study Quiz				
SNAP Concepts	Quiz				
SNAP Skill Items	Quiz				
SNAP PE	Comprehensive Performance Evaluation				

Chapter 3 Formatting Slides

Assignment	Title	Start from Scratch	SNAP Grade It	Date Due	Grade
Concepts Check			✓		
Skills Check Assessment 1	Create, Format, and Modify a Benefits Presentation	✓	✓		
Skills Check Assessment 2	Format and Modify a Perennials Presentation		✓		
Skills Check Assessment 3	Create and Apply a Custom Theme to a Travel Presentation	✓	✓		

Assignment	Title	Start from Scratch	SNAP Grade It	Date Due	Grade
Skills Check Assessment 4	Prepare a Presentation on Online Shopping				
Visual Benchmark	Format a Presentation on Home Safety				
Case Study Part 1	La Dolce Vita: Lunch Menu Presentation	✓			
Case Study Part 2	La Dolce Vita: Formatting Lunch Menu Presentation				
Case Study Part 3	La Dolce Vita: Restaurant Menu Printers Presentation (Internet)	✓			
Case Study Part 4	La Dolce Vita: Hyperlinking in Presentation (Help)	✓			
SNAP Tutorial 3.1	Applying Formatting Using the Font Group				
SNAP Tutorial 3.2	Applying Formatting Using the Font Dialog Box				
SNAP Tutorial 3.3	Formatting with Format Painter				
SNAP Tutorial 3.4	Changing Paragraph Formatting				
SNAP Tutorial 3.5	Customizing Bullets and Numbering				
SNAP Tutorial 3.6	Customizing Placeholders				
SNAP Tutorial 3.7	Changing Page Setup				
SNAP Tutorial 3.8	Changing Slide Size, Design Themes, and Background Styles				
SNAP Tutorial 3.9	Creating and Deleting Custom Themes				
IRC Quiz	Study Quiz				
SNAP Concepts	Quiz				
SNAP Skill Items	Quiz				
SNAP PE	Comprehensive Performance Evaluation				

Chapter 4 Inserting Elements in Slides

Assignment	Title	Start from Scratch	SNAP Grade It	Date Due	Grade
Concepts Check			✓		
Skills Check Assessment 1	Format and Add Enhancements to a Travel Presentation		✓		
Skills Check Assessment 2	Format and Add Enhancements to a Gardening Presentation		✓		
Skills Check Assessment 3	Copy a Picture from a Website to a Presentation				
Visual Benchmark	Creating a Study Abroad Presentation	✓			

Assignment	Title	Start from Scratch	SNAP Grade It	Date Due	Grade
Case Study Part 1	Honoré Financial Services: Community Workshop Presentation	✓			
Case Study Part 2	Honoré Financial Services: Financial Planning Presentation	✓			
Case Study Part 3	Honoré Financial Services: Workshop Flyer	✓			
Case Study Part 4	Honoré Financial Services: Hyperlinks in a Presentation (Internet)	✓			
SNAP Tutorial 4.1	Displaying Gridlines; Inserting a Text Box; Copying and Rotating Shapes				
SNAP Tutorial 4.2	Formatting a Text Box				
SNAP Tutorial 4.3	Drawing and Customizing Shapes				
SNAP Tutorial 4.4	Grouping/Ungrouping Objects				
SNAP Tutorial 4.5	Inserting and Formatting Images				
SNAP Tutorial 4.6	Inserting and Formatting Clip Art Images				
SNAP Tutorial 4.7	Creating and Inserting Screenshots				
SNAP Tutorial 4.8	Inserting and Formatting WordArt				
SNAP Tutorial 4.9	Inserting Headers and Footers				

Unit 1 Performance Assessments

Assignment	Title	Start from Scratch	SNAP Grade It	Date Due	Grade
Assessment 1	Prepare, Format, and Enhance a Conference Presentation	✓			
Assessment 2	Format and Enhance a Kraft Artworks Presentation				
Assessment 3	Create and Apply a Custom Theme to a Job Search Presentation	✓			
Assessment 4	Format and Enhance a Medical Plans Presentation				
Writing Activity 1	Prepare and Format a Health Plan Presentation	✓			
Writing Activity 2	Prepare and Format a Presentation on Saving an Image as a JPG	✓			
Internet Research	Analyze a Magazine Website	✓			
Supplemental Assessment 1	Create a Presentation	✓			
Supplemental Assessment 2	Format and Insert Transitions to a Presentation	✓			
SNAP PE	Comprehensive Performance Evaluation				

Assignment	Title	Start from Scratch	SNAP Grade It	Date Due	Grade
Unit 2: Customizing and Enhancing PowerPoint Presentations					

Chapter 5 Creating Tables, Charts, and SmartArt Graphics

Assignment	Title	Start from Scratch	SNAP Grade It	Date Due	Grade
Concepts Check			✓		
Skills Check Assessment 1	Create and Format Tables and SmartArt in a Restaurant Presentation		✓		
Skills Check Assessment 2	Create and Format Charts in a Marketing Presentation		✓		
Skills Check Assessment 3	Create a Scenery Photo Album	✓	✓		
Skills Check Assessment 4	Create a Sales Area Chart				
Visual Benchmark	Create and Format a Medical Center Presentation				
Case Study Part 1	Terra Energy Corporation: Quarterly Meeting Presentation	✓			
Case Study Part 2	Terra Energy Corporation: Adding SmartArt				
Case Study Part 3	Terra Energy Corporation: Adding Department Costs	✓			
SNAP Tutorial 5.1	Creating a Table in a Slide				
SNAP Tutorial 5.2	Inserting and Formatting and Excel Spreadsheet				
SNAP Tutorial 5.3	Inserting and Formatting SmartArt				
SNAP Tutorial 5.4	Converting SmartArt to Text and to Shapes				
SNAP Tutorial 5.5	Creating and Formatting Charts				
SNAP Tutorial 5.6	Creating a Photo Album				
IRC Quiz	Study Quiz				
SNAP Concepts	Quiz				
SNAP Skill Items	Quiz				
SNAP PE	Comprehensive Performance Evaluation				

Chapter 6 Using Slide Masters and Action Buttons

Assignment	Title	Start from Scratch	SNAP Grade It	Date Due	Grade
Concepts Check			✓		
Skills Check Assessment 1	Format a Presentation in Slide Master View and Then Save the Presentation as a Template	✓	✓		

Assignment	Title	Start from Scratch	SNAP Grade It	Date Due	Grade
Skills Check Assessment 2	Use a Template to Create a Publications Presentation	✓	✓		
Skills Check Assessment 3	Insert Action Buttons in a Gardening Presentation		✓		
Skills Check Assessment 4	Create an Action Buttons Presentation	✓			
Visual Benchmark	Create and Format a Company Branch Office Presentation	✓			
Case Study Part 1	Anchor Corporation: New Employee Orientation	✓			
Case Study Part 2	Anchor Corporation: Employee Information Presentation	✓			
Case Study Part 3	Anchor Corporation: Guidelines Presentation				
Case Study Part 4	Anchor Corporation: Employee Classifications Presentation				
Case Study Part 5	Anchor Corporation: Linking a Presentation to a Word Document				
SNAP Tutorial 6.1	Formatting with a Slide Master				
SNAP Tutorial 6.2	Working in Slide Master View				
SNAP Tutorial 6.3	Saving a Presentation as a Template				
SNAP Tutorial 6.4	Customizing a Handout and Notes Master				
SNAP Tutorial 6.5	Using VIEW Tab Options				
SNAP Tutorial 6.6	Inserting Action Buttons and Hyperlinks				
IRC Quiz	Study Quiz				
SNAP Concepts	Quiz				
SNAP Skill Items	Quiz				
SNAP PE	Comprehensive Performance Evaluation				

Chapter 7 Applying Custom Animation and Setting Up Shows

Concepts Check			✓		
Skills Check Assessment 1	Apply Animation Effects to a Travel Presentation		✓		
Skills Check Assessment 2	Apply Animation Effects to An Employee Orientation Presentation		✓		
Skills Check Assessment 3	Apply Animation Effects, Video, and Audio to a Job Search Presentation		✓		

Assignment	Title	Start from Scratch	SNAP Grade It	Date Due	Grade
Skills Check Assessment 4	Insert an Audio File from Office. com				
Visual Benchmark	Create and Format a Medical Center Presentation				
Case Study Part 1	Summit Services: Purchasing a Personal Computer Presentation	✓			
Case Study Part 2	Summit Services: Creating Custom Show				
Case Study Part 3	Summit Services: Adding Audio File (Internet)				
SNAP Tutorial 7.1	Applying Animation to Objects and Text				
SNAP Tutorial 7.2	Animating Shapes, Images, SmartArt, and Chart Elements				
SNAP Tutorial 7.3	Setting Up a Slide Show				
SNAP Tutorial 7.4	Applying Sound to Animations				
SNAP Tutorial 7.5	Setting Timings for a Presentation				
SNAP Tutorial 7.6	Creating and Running a Custom Show				
SNAP Tutorial 7.7	Adding Audio and Video				
SNAP Tutorial 7.8	Modifying Audio and Video Files				
IRC Quiz	Study Quiz				
SNAP Concepts	Quiz				
SNAP Skill Items	Quiz				
SNAP PE	Comprehensive Performance Evaluation				

Chapter 8 Integrating, Sharing, and Protecting Presentations

Assignment	Title	Start from Scratch	SNAP Grade It	Date Due	Grade
Concepts Check			✓		
Skills Check Assessment 1	Copy Word and Excel Data into a Sales Conference Presentation				
Skills Check Assessment 2	Copy and Link Word and Excel Data into a Communications Presentation				
Skills Check Assessment 3	Save a Sales Conference Presentation in Various Formats		✓		
Skills Check Assessment 4	Download and Fill in an Award Certificate	✓			
Visual Benchmark 1	Create JPEG Image Files and Create a Word Document				
Visual Benchmark 2	Create a Travel Company Presentation	✓			

Assignment	Title	Start from Scratch	SNAP Grade It	Date Due	Grade
Case Study Part 1	Rocky Mountain Family Medicine: Insert a Logo into a Presentation				
Case Study Part 2	Rocky Mountain Family Medicine: Childhood Diseases Presentation				
Case Study Part 3	Rocky Mountain Family Medicine: Education and Training Presentation				
Case Study Part 4	Rocky Mountain Family Medicine: Measles Presentation (Internet)				
SNAP Tutorial 8.1	Integrating with Word and Excel				
SNAP Tutorial 8.2	Exporting Presentations				
SNAP Tutorial 8.3	Saving a Presentation in a Different Format				
SNAP Tutorial 8.4	Embedding and Linking Objects				
SNAP Tutorial 8.5	Downloading and Applying a Design Template				
SNAP Tutorial 8.6	Comparing and Combining Presentations; Inserting and Deleting Comments				
SNAP Tutorial 8.7	Managing Presentation Information and Properties				
SNAP Tutorial 8.8	Customizing PowerPoint Options				
IRC Quiz	Study Quiz				
SNAP Concepts	Quiz				
SNAP Skill Items	Quiz				
SNAP PE	Comprehensive Performance Evaluation				

Unit 2 Performance Assessments

Assignment	Title	Start from Scratch	SNAP Grade It	Date Due	Grade
Assessment 1	Save and Insert a Slide in JPEG Format, Format a Slide Master, Create a Table and SmartArt Graphics, and Insert Comments				
Assessment 2	Copy and Paste Data between Programs and Insert Action Buttons in a Travel Presentation				
Assessment 3	Save a Template Presentation and Copy, Embed, and Link Objects between Programs				
Assessment 4	Apply Custom Animation Effects to a Travel Presentation				
Assessment 5	Inspect a Presentation and Save a Presentation in Different Formats				

Assignment	Title	Start from Scratch	SNAP Grade It	Date Due	Grade
Writing Activity 1	Prepare and Format a Travel Presentation				
Writing Activity 2	Prepare and Format a Presentation on Media Files	✓			
Internet Research	Presenting Office 2013	✓			
Job Study	Creating a Skills Presentation	✓			
Supplemental Assessment 1	IRA Presentation				
Supplemental Assessment 2	Revise an IRA Presentation				
Final Case Study	Lambton Logistics				
SNAP PE	Comprehensive Performance Evaluation				

Concepts Check Answer Key
Benchmark PowerPoint 2013, Chapter 1

1.	Click this tab to display tabs and buttons for working with presentations.	FILE tab	page 6 (Table 1.1)
2.	This toolbar contains buttons for commonly used commands.	Quick Access	page 6 (Table 1.1)
3.	This area contains the tabs and commands divided into groups.	ribbon	page 6 (Table 1.1)
4.	This is the keyboard shortcut to close a presentation.	Ctrl + F4	page 8
5.	Display design theme templates in this backstage area.	New	page 10
6.	Insert a new slide by clicking the New Slide button in this group on the HOME tab.	Slides	page 12
7.	Change to this view to view displays of all slides in the presentation in slide thumbnails.	Slide Sorter	page 16
8.	This is the default view and displays two panes.	Normal	page 16
9.	Click this button on the VIEW tab to display the outline pane.	Outline View	page 16
10.	The Previous Slide and Next Slide buttons display in this location.	bottom of the vertical scroll bar	page 16
11.	To run a presentation beginning with Slide 1, click this button on the Quick Access toolbar.	Start From Beginning	page 22
12.	Apply a theme to a presentation by clicking this tab and then clicking the desired theme in the Themes group.	DESIGN	page 27
13.	To add a transition, click a transition thumbnail in the Transition to This Slide group on this tab.	TRANSITIONS	page 31
14.	When you apply a transition to slides in a presentation, these display below the slide numbers in the slide thumbnails pane.	animation icons	page 32
15.	To advance slides automatically, remove the check mark from the *On Mouse Click* check box, insert a check mark in this check box, and then insert the desired number of seconds.	*After*	page 34

Concepts Check Answer Key
Benchmark PowerPoint 2013, Chapter 2

1.	The Spelling button is located in the Proofing group on this tab.	REVIEW	page 45
2.	This is the keyboard shortcut to select all text in a placeholder.	Ctrl + A	page 48 (Table 2.2)
3.	The Find button is located in this group on the HOME tab.	Editing	page 49
4.	To copy text to a new location in the slide thumbnails pane, hold down this key while dragging text.	Ctrl	page 55
5.	The border of a selected placeholder displays these handles as well as a white rotation handle.	sizing	page 55
6.	You can reorganize slides in a presentation in the slide thumbnails pane or in this view.	Slide Sorter	page 57
7.	You can copy selected slides in a presentation using this option from the New Slide button drop-down list.	*Duplicate Selected Slides*	page 60
8.	To select adjacent slides, click the first slide, hold down this key, and then click the last slide.	Shift	page 60
9.	Click the New Slide button arrow and then click the *Reuse Slides* option at the drop-down list to display this.	Reuse Slides task pane	page 61
10.	Divide a presentation into these to easily navigate and edit slides in a presentation.	sections	page 63
11.	Display the Quick Access toolbar below the ribbon by clicking this button located at the right side of the toolbar and then clicking the *Show Below the Ribbon* option at the drop-down list.	Customize Quick Access Toolbar	page 65
12.	This is the keyboard shortcut to display the PowerPoint Help window.	F1	page 67

Concepts Check Answer Key
Benchmark PowerPoint 2013, Chapter 3

1.	The Font button drop-down gallery is an example of this feature, which allows you to see how formatting will affect your text before you actually apply it.	live preview	page 81
2.	Click this button to clear character formatting from selected text.	Clear All Formatting	page 82 (Table 3.1)
3.	Click this to display the Font dialog box.	Font group dialog box launcher	page 82
4.	Select text in a slide and this displays above the selected text.	Mini toolbar	page 83
5.	The Format Painter button is located in this group on the HOME tab.	Clipboard	page 85
6.	Press this key to move text to the next tab stop (level).	Tab	page 87 (Table 3.2)
7.	Use options at this dialog box to change text alignment, indentation, and spacing.	Paragraph	page 90
8.	Click this button in the Paragraph group and a drop-down list displays with options for rotating and stacking text.	Text Direction	page 92
9.	Use the Align Text button or options at this task pane with the Size & Properties icon selected to vertically align text in a slide.	Format Shape	page 92
10.	Customize numbering with options at the Bullets and Numbering dialog box with this tab selected.	Numbered	page 96
11.	The Quick Styles button is located in this group on the HOME tab.	Drawing	page 98
12.	Click this button to apply an outline to a placeholder.	Shape Outline	page 98
13.	Change slide orientation with options in this dialog box.	Slide Size	Page 103
14.	Click this button in the Customize group on the DESIGN tab to display the Format Background task pane.	Format Background	Page 105
15.	Create custom theme colors with options at this dialog box.	Create New Theme Colors	page 109
16.	Save a custom theme at this dialog box.	Save Current Theme	page 112

Concepts Check Answer Key
Benchmark PowerPoint 2013, Chapter 4

1.	The Text Box button is located in the Text group on this tab.	INSERT	page 126
2.	Use the sizing handles or these measurement boxes to change the size of a text box.	*Shape Height* and *Shape Width*	page 127
3.	This is the keyboard shortcut to select all objects in a slide.	Ctrl + A	page 127
4.	A text box, by default, contains tabs with this alignment.	left	page 133
5.	The Illustrations group on this tab contains a shapes button.	INSERT	page 135
6.	When dragging a shape to change the size, hold down this key to maintain the proportions of the shape.	Shift	page 135
7.	Copy a shape by holding down this key while dragging the shape to the desired location.	Ctrl	page 136
8.	Turn drawing guides on and off with options in this dialog box.	Grid and Guides	page 136
9.	The Group button is located in this group on the DRAWING TOOLS FORMAT tab.	Arrange	page 141
10.	Click the Online Pictures button and this window displays	Insert Pictures	page 149
11.	Use this button in the Size group on the PICTURE TOOLS FORMAT tab to remove any unnecessary parts of an image.	Crop	page 143
12.	With the Bring Forward button and this button in the Arrange group on the DRAWING TOOLS FORMAT tab or the PICTURE TOOLS FORMAT tab you can layer one object on top of another.	Send Backward	page 143
13.	To capture a portion of a screen, click the Screenshot button in the Images group on the INSERT tab and then click this option at the drop-down list.	*Screen Clipping*	page 153
14.	Use this feature to distort or modify text to conform to a variety of shapes.	WordArt	page 154
15.	The Symbol button is located in the Symbols group on this tab.	INSERT	page 156
16.	Click this hyperlink at the Print backstage area to display the Header and Footer dialog box.	Edit Header & Footer	page 157

Concepts Check Answer Key
Benchmark PowerPoint 2013, Chapter 5

1.	This term refers to the intersection between a row and a column.	cell	page 189
2.	Display the Insert Table dialog box by clicking this button in a content placeholder.	Insert Table	page 189
3.	Press this key on the keyboard to move the insertion point to the next cell.	Tab	page 189
4.	Press these keys on the keyboard to select all cells in a table.	Ctrl + A	page 190 (Table 5.1)
5.	The Table Styles group is located on this tab.	TABLE TOOLS DESIGN	page 191
6.	Use options and buttons on this tab to delete and insert rows and columns and merge and split cells.	TABLE TOOLS LAYOUT	page 193
7.	Click this button in a content placeholder to display the Choose a SmartArt Graphic dialog box.	Insert SmartArt Graphic	page 198
8.	When you insert a SmartArt diagram in a slide, this tab is active.	SMARTART TOOLS DESIGN	page 199
9.	Create a SmartArt diagram with bulleted text by clicking in the text placeholder, clicking this button, and then clicking the desired SmartArt graphic at the drop-down gallery.	Convert to SmartArt Graphic (or Convert to SmartArt)	page 203
10.	Click the Chart button in this group on the INSERT tab to display the Insert Chart dialog box.	Illustrations	page 206
11.	Insert a chart in a slide and this tab is active.	CHART TOOLS DESIGN	page 210
12.	To edit data in a chart, click the Edit Data button in this group on the CHART TOOLS DESIGN tab.	Data	page 211
13.	This group on the CHART TOOLS FORMAT tab contains predesigned styles you can apply to shapes in a chart.	Shape Styles	page 213
14.	This group on the CHART TOOLS FORMAT tab contains predesigned styles you can apply to chart text.	WordArt Styles	page 213

15.	To create a photo album, click the INSERT tab, click the Photo Album button arrow, and then click this at the drop-down list.	*New Photo Album*	page 217
16.	Click the down-pointing arrow at the right of this option in the Edit Photo Album dialog box to display a list of framing choices.	*Frame shape*	page 219
17.	To insert captions below pictures in a photo album, insert a check mark in this check box in the Edit Photo Album dialog box.	*Captions below ALL pictures*	page 219

Concepts Check Answer Key
Benchmark PowerPoint 2013, Chapter 6

1.	To display a presentation in Slide Master view, click this tab and then click the Slide Master button.	VIEW	page 237
2.	Click this button to close Slide Master view.	Close Master View	page 238
3.	This group on the SLIDE MASTER tab contains buttons for applying theme colors and theme fonts.	Edit Theme	page 238
4.	This dialog box with the Slide tab selected contains options for inserting the date and time, a slide number, and a footer.	Header and Footer	page 243
5.	To create a new slide layout in Slide Master view, click this button in the Edit Master group.	Insert Layout	page 244
6.	To save a presentation as a template, choose this option at the *Save as type* option drop-down list in the Save As dialog box.	*PowerPoint Template (*.potx)*	page 250
7.	Change to this view to customize handouts.	Handout Master	page 251
8.	Change to this view to customize notes pages.	Notes Master	page 253
9.	The Zoom slider bar is located at the right side of this bar.	Status	page 255
10.	Click this button to display a drop-down list that includes action buttons.	Shapes	page 258
11.	Insert this action button in a slide to display the next slide in the presentation.	Forward or Next	page 259
12.	Insert this action button in a slide to display the first slide in the presentation.	Home	page 260
13.	This is the keyboard shortcut to display the Insert Hyperlink dialog box.	Ctrl + K	page 262

Concepts Check Answer Key
Benchmark PowerPoint 2013, Chapter 7

1.	Once you have applied an animation, specify the animation effects with options in this button drop-down gallery.	Effect Options	page 278
2.	Remove an animation effect from an item in a slide by clicking this option in the Animation group on the ANIMATIONS tab.	*None*	page 280
3.	The Add Animation button in the Advanced Animation group on the ANIMATIONS tab provides four types of animation effects you can apply to an item—entrance, exit, motion paths, and this.	emphasis	page 281
4.	Use this feature if you apply an animation or animations to items in a slide and want to apply the same animation in more than one location in a slide or slides.	Animation Painter	page 281
5.	The *Duration* measurement box is located in this group on the ANIMATIONS tab.	Timing	page 283
6.	Display the Animation Pane by clicking the Animation Pane button in this group on the ANIMATIONS tab.	Advanced Animation	page 285
7.	This term refers to displaying important points one at a time in a slide when running a presentation.	build	page 288
8.	To draw your own motion path in a slide, click the Add Animation button on the ANIMATIONS tab and then click this option in the *Motion Paths* section of the drop-down gallery.	*Custom Path*	page 293
9.	The Hide Slide button is located on this tab.	SLIDE SHOW	page 302
10.	Specify the slides you want included in a custom show with options at this dialog box.	Define Custom Show	page 306
11.	The Audio and Video buttons are located in this group on the INSERT tab.	Media	page 308
12.	The Volume button for an audio file is located in the Audio Options group on this tab.	AUDIO TOOLS PLAYBACK	page 309 (Fig. 7.6)
13.	The Trim Video button is located on this tab.	VIDEO TOOLS PLAYBACK	page 313

Concepts Check Answer Key
Benchmark PowerPoint 2013, Chapter 8

1.	Display the Insert Outline dialog box by clicking the New Slide button arrow and then clicking this option.	*Slides from Outline*	page 328
2.	Use this task pane to collect and paste multiple items.	Clipboard	page 330
3.	The *Invite People* option is available at this backstage area.	Share	page 331
4.	If you save the presentation in PDF format, the presentation opens in this.	Adobe Reader	page 334
5.	With this option at the Export backstage area, you can export a PowerPoint presentation to a Word document.	Create Handouts	page 336
6.	A presentation you save as a PowerPoint Show will display with this file extension.	.ppsx	page 339
7.	With options in the *Image File Types* section of the Export backstage area with the *Change File Type* option selected, you can save slides in a presentation as graphic images as JPEG files or this type of file.	PNG	page 341
8.	Do this to an object if you want the contents in the destination program to reflect any changes made to the object stored in the source program.	Link	page 344
9.	Download a template at this backstage area.	New	page 346
10.	Click the Merge button at the Choose File to Merge with Current Presentation dialog box when comparing presentations and this task pane displays.	Reviewing	page 349
11.	The New Comment button is located in the Comments group on this tab.	REVIEW	page 351
12.	Display additional presentation properties at the Info backstage area by clicking this hyperlink.	Show All Properties	page 354
13.	Display the Encrypt Document dialog box by clicking the FILE tab, clicking the Protect Presentation button at the Info backstage area, and then clicking this option at the drop-down list.	*Encrypt with Password*	page 356
14.	Use this feature to inspect your presentation for personal data, hidden data, and metadata.	document inspector	page 358
15.	Use this feature to check a presentation for content that a person with a visual impairment might find difficult to read.	accessibility checker	page 359
16.	Use this button at the Info backstage area to open an autosaved backup presentation.	Manage Versions	page 361
17.	Customize PowerPoint with options at this dialog box.	PowerPoint Options	page 362

PowerPoint Chapter 1 Model Answers

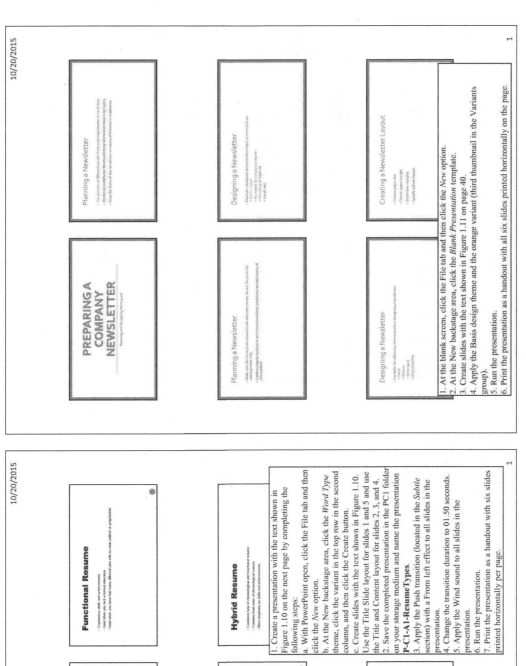

P-C1-A2-Newsletter(A2,Step6).pptx

P-C1-A1-ResumeTypes(A1).pptx

Benchmark PowerPoint 2013 Model Answers

P-C1-VB-Interview(VB).pptx

P-C1-A2-Newsletter(A2,Step9).pptx

10/20/2015

10/20/2015

7. make the following changes to the presentation:
a. Apply the Parallax design theme and the red variant (fourth thumbnail in the *Variants* group).
b. Add the Switch transition (located in the *Exciting* section) with a left effect to all slides.
c. Add the Camera sound to all slides.
d. Specify that all slides advance automatically after five seconds.
8. Run the presentation.

HOME SAFETY: SMOKE DETECTORS

BY: STUDENT NAME

TYPES OF SMOKE DETECTORS

- Most common detectors are:
  - Ionization – sensitive to detect heat and fires that emit minimal smoke.
  - Photoelectric – can detect particles in the air through infrared LED.

P-C1-CS-PPSmokeDetectors(CS2).pptx (1 of 3)

P-C1-CS-PPSmokeDetectors(CS1).pptx

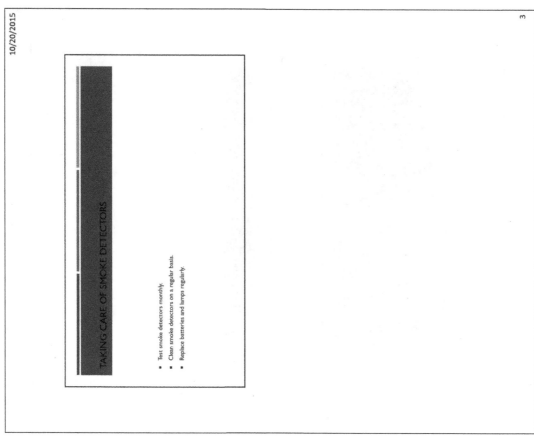

TAKING CARE OF SMOKE DETECTORS

- Test smoke detectors monthly.
- Clean smoke detectors on a regular basis.
- Replace batteries and lamps regularly.

P-C1-CS-PPSmokeDetectors(CS2).pptx (3 of 3)

DEVELOPING AN ESCAPE PLAN

- Draw a floor plan of the home that identifies at least two methods of escape from every room.
- Practice evacuating the home while blindfolded.
- Practice staying low to the ground while escaping.
- Practice stopping, dropping to the ground, and rolling.
- Identify a safe meeting place outside the home.
- Practice alerting other members of the household.

SAFETY TIPS

- Develop an escape plan.
- Post emergency numbers by the phone.
- Practice locating and use of ladders and fire extinguishers.
- Keep stove and kitchen areas clean and uncluttered.
- Do not overload outlets or use ragged electrical wiring.

P-C1-CS-PPSmokeDetectors(CS2).pptx (2 of 3)

1. **HOME SAFETY: SMOKE DETECTORS**
   BY: STUDENT NAME

2. **TYPES OF SMOKE DETECTORS**
   - Most common detectors are:
     - Ionization – sensitive to detect heat and fires that emit minimal smoke.
     - Photoelectric – can detect particles in the air through infrared LED.

3. **DEVELOPING AN ESCAPE PLAN**
   - Draw a floor plan of the home that identifies at least two methods of escape from every room.
     - Practice evacuating the home while blindfolded.
     - Practice staying low to the ground while escaping.
     - Practice stopping, dropping to the ground, and rolling.
     - Identify a safe meeting place outside the home.
     - Practice alerting other members of the household.

4. **SAFETY TIPS**
   - Develop an escape plan.
   - Post emergency numbers by the phone.
   - Practice locating and use of ladders and fire extinguishers.
   - Keep stove and kitchen areas clean and uncluttered.
   - Do not overload outlets or use ragged electrical wiring.

5. **TAKING CARE OF SMOKE DETECTORS**
   - Test smoke detectors monthly.
   - Clean smoke detectors on a regular basis.
   - Replace batteries and lamps regularly.

6. **WHERE TO PURCHASE A SMOKE DETECTOR**
   - Kidde Smoke Alarms – www.smokealarms.kidde.com
   - First Alert – www.firstalert.com/wheretobuy
   - Wide selection of Smoke Detectors – www.homedepot.com

1

P-C1-CS-PPSmokeDetectors(CS3).pptx

PowerPoint Chapter 2 Model Answers

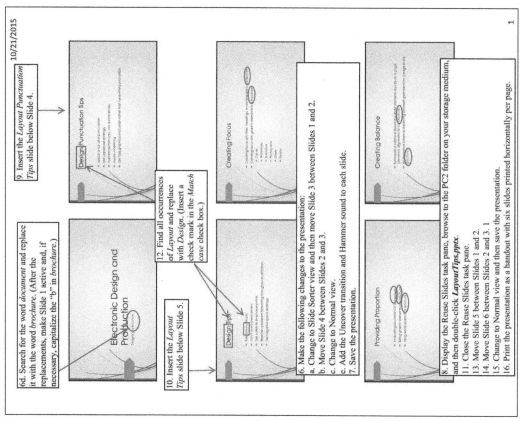

10/21/2015

9. Insert the *Layout Punctuation Tips* slide below Slide 4.

6d. Search for the word *document* and replace it with the word *brochure*. (After the replacements, make Slide 1 active and, if necessary, capitalize the "b" in *brochure*.)

12. Find all occurrences of *Layout* and replace with *Design*. (Insert a check mark in the *Match case* check box.)

10. Insert the *Layout Tips* slide below Slide 5.

6. Make the following changes to the presentation:
a. Change to Slide Sorter view and then move Slide 3 between Slides 1 and 2.
b. Move Slide 4 between Slides 2 and 3.
c. Change to Normal view.
c. Add the Uncover transition and Hammer sound to each slide.
7. Save the presentation.

8. Display the Reuse Slides task pane, browse to the PC2 folder on your storage medium, and then double-click **LayoutTips.pptx**.
11. Close the Reuse Slides task pane.
13. Move Slide 5 between Slides 1 and 2.
14. Move Slide 6 between Slides 2 and 3. 1
15. Change to Normal view and then save the presentation.
16. Print the presentation as a handout with six slides printed horizontally per page.

P-C2-A1-ElecDesign(A1,Step16).pptx

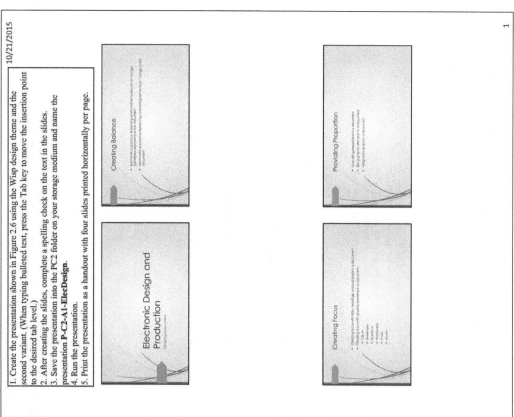

10/21/2015

1. Create the presentation shown in Figure 2.6 using the Wisp design theme and the second variant. (When typing bulleted text, press the Tab key to move the insertion point to the desired tab level.)
2. After creating the slides, complete a spelling check on the text in the slides.
3. Save the presentation into the PC2 folder on your storage medium and name the presentation **P-C2-A1-ElecDesign**.
4. Run the presentation.
5. Print the presentation as a handout with four slides printed horizontally per page.

P-C2-A1-ElecDesign(A1,Step5).pptx

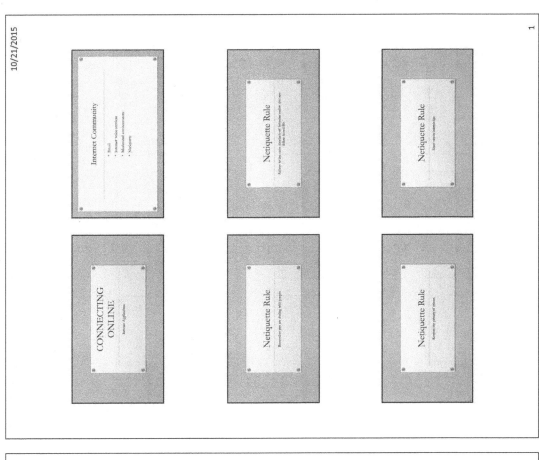

P-C2-A1-ElecDesign(A1,Step19).pptx

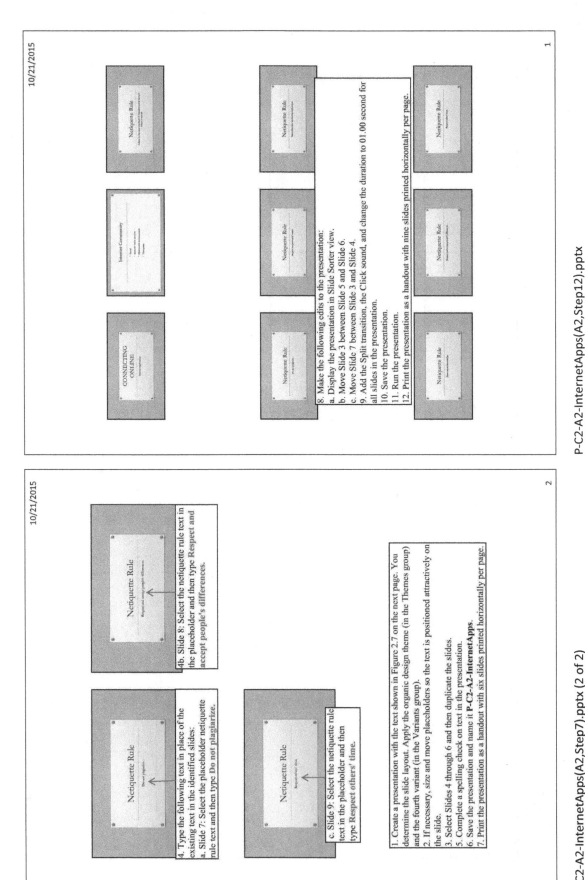

8. Make the following edits to the presentation:
   a. Display the presentation in Slide Sorter view.
   b. Move Slide 3 between Slide 5 and Slide 6.
   c. Move Slide 7 between Slide 3 and Slide 4.
9. Add the Split transition, the Click sound, and change the duration to 01.00 second for all slides in the presentation.
10. Save the presentation.
11. Run the presentation.
12. Print the presentation as a handout with nine slides printed horizontally per page.

P-C2-A2-InternetApps(A2,Step12).pptx

4b. Slide 8: Select the netiquette rule text in the placeholder and then type Respect and accept people's differences.

4. Type the following text in place of the existing text in the identified slides:
   a. Slide 7: Select the placeholder netiquette rule text and then type Do not plagiarize.

c. Slide 9: Select the netiquette rule text in the placeholder and then type Respect others' time.

1. Create a presentation with the text shown in Figure 2.7 on the next page. You determine the slide layout. Apply the organic design theme (in the Themes group) and the fourth variant (in the Variants group).
2. If necessary, size and move placeholders so the text is positioned attractively on the slide.
3. Select Slides 4 through 6 and then duplicate the slides.
5. Complete a spelling check on text in the presentation.
6. Save the presentation and name it P-C2-A2-InternetApps.
7. Print the presentation as a handout with six slides printed horizontally per page.

P-C2-A2-InternetApps(A2,Step7).pptx (2 of 2)

Benchmark PowerPoint 2013 Model Answers

P-C2-CS-JobAnalysis(CS3).pptx (1 of 2)

P-C2-A3-VB-OnlineLearning(VB).pptx

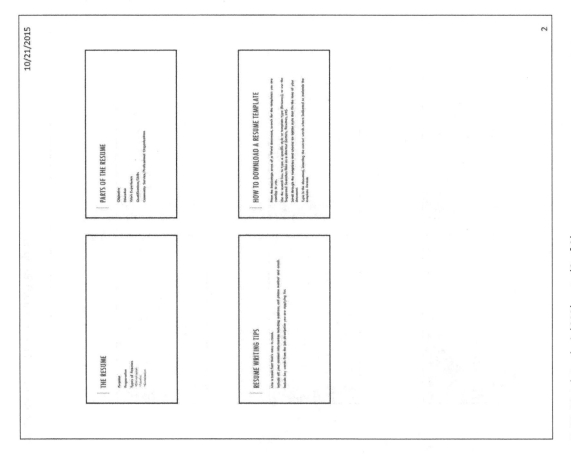

PowerPoint Chapter 3 Model Answers

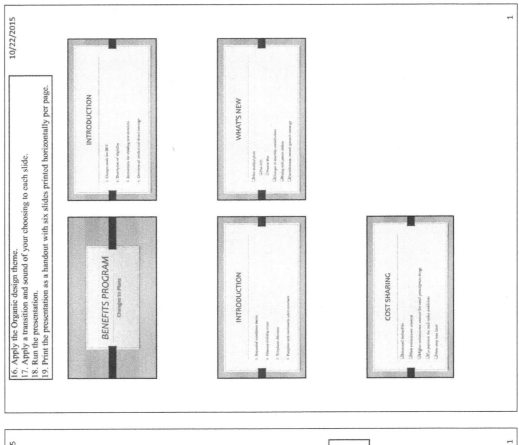

P-C3-A1-Benefits(A1,Step20).pptx

P-C3-A1-Benefits(A1,Step15).pptx

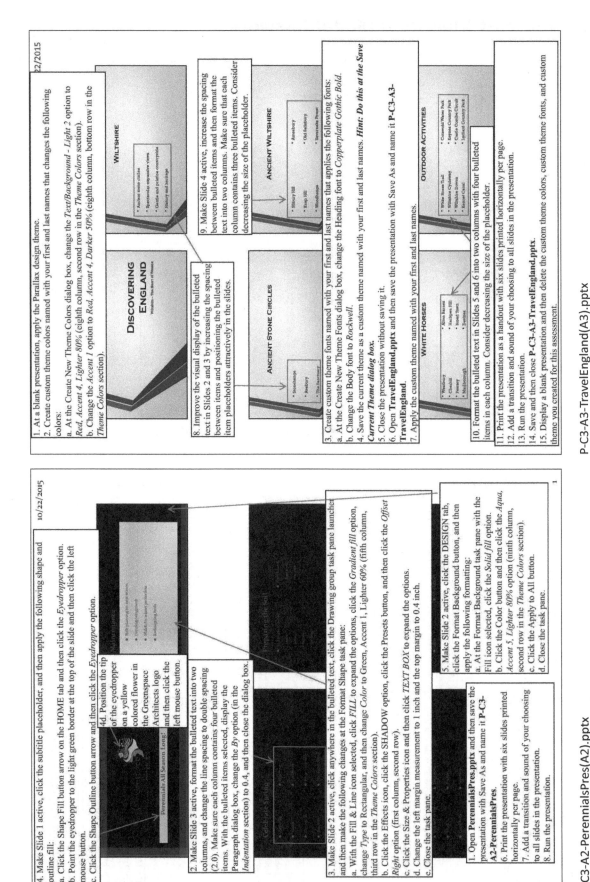

P-C3-A3-TravelEngland(A3).pptx

22/2015

1. At a blank presentation, apply the Parallax design theme.
2. Create custom theme colors named with your first and last names that changes the following colors:
   a. At the Create New Theme Colors dialog box, change the *Text/Background - Light 2* option to *Red, Accent 4, Lighter 80%* (eighth column, second row in the *Theme Colors* section).
   b. Change the *Accent 1* option to *Red, Accent 4, Darker 50%* (eighth column, bottom row in the *Theme Colors* section).

8. Improve the visual display of the bulleted text in Slides 2 and 3 by increasing the spacing between items and positioning the bulleted item placeholders attractively in the slides.

9. Make Slide 4 active, increase the spacing between bulleted items and then format the text into two columns. Make sure that each column contains three bulleted items. Consider decreasing the size of the placeholder.

3. Create custom theme fonts named with your first and last names that applies the following fonts:
   a. At the Create New Theme Fonts dialog box, change the Heading font to *Copperplate Gothic Bold*.
   b. Change the Body font to *Rockwell*.
4. Save the current theme as a custom theme named with your first and last names. *Hint: Do this at the Save Current Theme dialog box.*
5. Close the presentation without saving it.
6. Open **TravelEngland.pptx** and then save the presentation with Save As and name it **P-C3-A3-TravelEngland**.
7. Apply the custom theme named with your first and last names.

10. Format the bulleted text in Slides 5 and 6 into two columns with four bulleted items in each column. Consider decreasing the size of the placeholder.
11. Print the presentation as a handout with six slides printed horizontally per page.
12. Add a transition and sound of your choosing to all slides in the presentation.
13. Run the presentation.
14. Save and then close **P-C3-A3-TravelEngland.pptx**.
15. Display a blank presentation and then delete the custom theme colors, custom theme fonts, and custom theme you created for this assessment.

P-C3-A2-PerennialsPres(A2).pptx

10/22/2015

4. Make Slide 1 active, click the subtitle placeholder, and then apply the following shape and outline fill:
   a. Click the Shape Fill button arrow on the HOME tab and then click the *Eyedropper* option.
   b. Point the eyedropper to the light green border at the top of the slide and then click the left mouse button.
   c. Click the Shape Outline button arrow and then click the *Eyedropper* option.
   4d. Position the tip of the eyedropper on a yellow colored flower in the Greenspace Architects logo and then click the left mouse button.

2. Make Slide 3 active, format the bulleted text into two columns, and change the line spacing to double spacing (2.0). Make sure each column contains four bulleted items. With the bulleted items selected, display the Paragraph dialog box, change the *By* option (in the *Indentation* section) to 0.4, and then close the dialog box.

3. Make Slide 2 active, click anywhere in the bulleted text, click the Drawing group task pane launcher and then make the following changes at the Format Shape task pane:
   a. With the Fill & Line icon selected, click *FILL* to expand the options, click the *Gradient-fill* option, change *Type* to Rectangular, and then change *Color* to Green, Accent 1, Lighter 60% (fifth column, third row in the *Theme Colors* section).
   b. Click the Effects icon, click the *SHADOW* option, click the Presets button, and then click the *Offset Right* option (first column, second row).
   c. Click the Size & Properties icon and then click *TEXT BOX* to expand the options.
   d. Change the left margin measurement to 1 inch and the top margin to 0.4 inch.
   e. Close the task pane.

5. Make Slide 2 active, click the DESIGN tab, click the Format Background button, and then apply the following formatting:
   a. At the Format Background task pane with the Fill icon selected, click the *Solid fill* option.
   b. Click the Color button and then click the *Aqua, Accent 5, Lighter 80%* option (ninth column, second row in the *Theme Colors* section).
   c. Click the Apply to All button.
   d. Close the task pane.

1. Open **PerennialsPres.pptx** and then save the presentation with Save As and name it **P-C3-A2-PerennialsPres**.
6. Print the presentation with six slides printed horizontally per page.
7. Add a transition and sound of your choosing to all slides in the presentation.
8. Run the presentation.

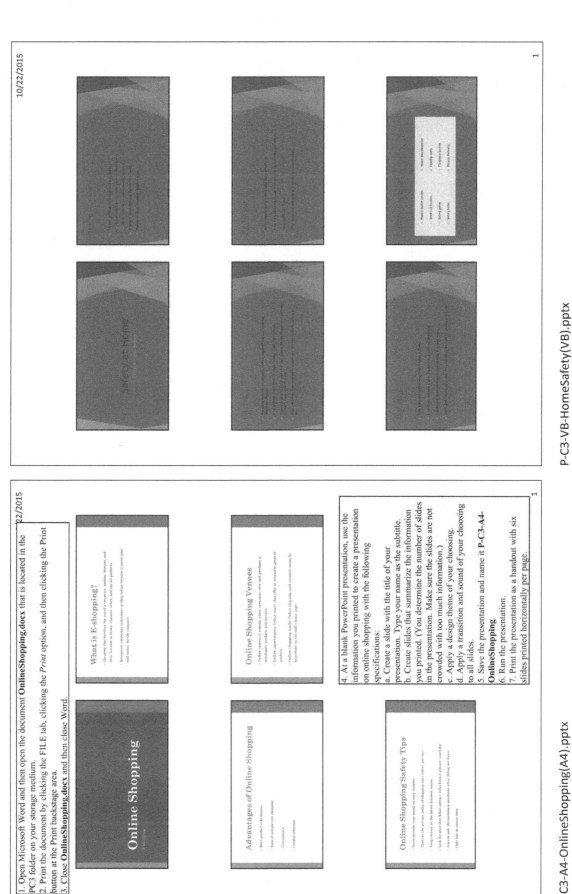

P-C3-CS-LunchMenu(CS2).pptx

P-C3-CS-LunchMenu(CS1).pptx

P-C3-CS-RestMenus(CS4).pptx

P-C3-CS-RestMenus(CS3).pptx

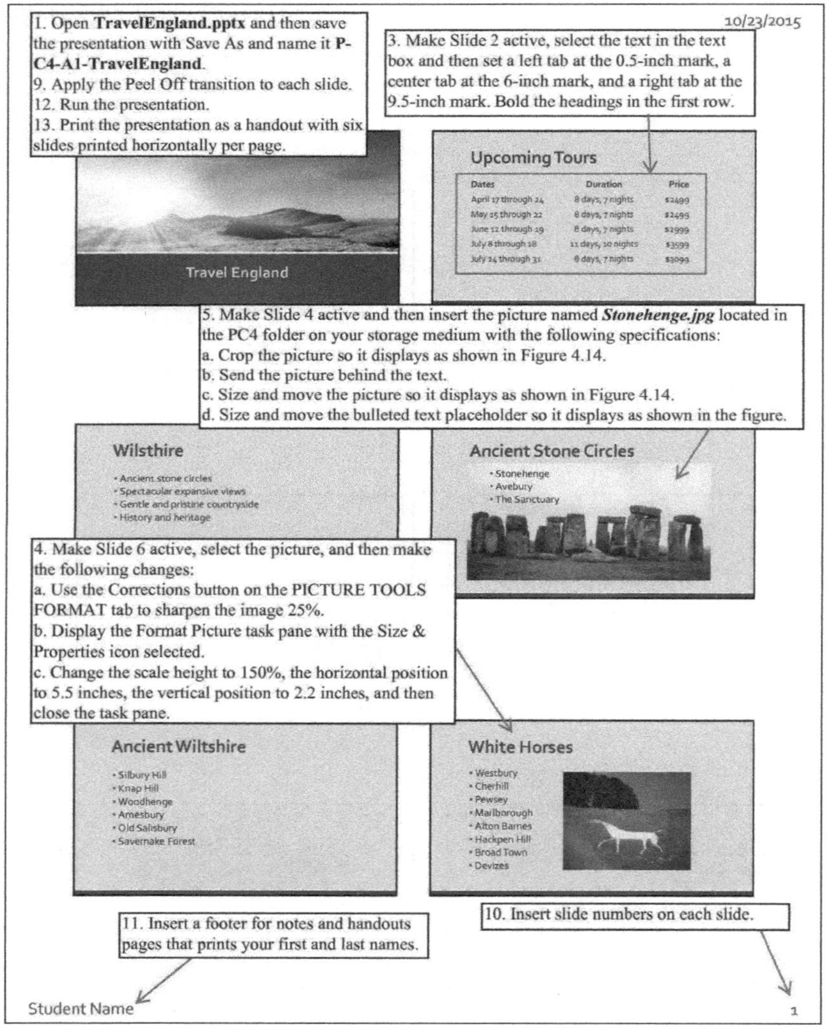

PowerPoint Chapter 4 Model Answers

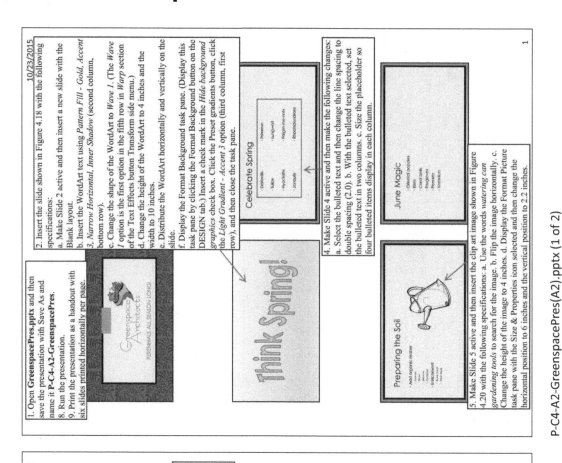

Greenspace Presentation (rotated layout):

10/23/2015

1. Open **GreenspacePres.pptx** and then save the presentation with Save As and name it **P-C4-A2-GreenspacePres**.
8. Run the presentation.
9. Print the presentation as a handout with six slides printed horizontally per page.

2. Insert the slide shown in Figure 4.18 with the following specifications:
   a. Make Slide 2 active and then insert a new slide with the Blank layout.
   b. Insert the WordArt text using *Pattern Fill - Gold, Accent 3, Narrow Horizontal, Inner Shadow* (second column, bottom row).
   c. Change the shape of the WordArt to *Wave 1*. (The *Wave 1* option is the first option in the fifth row in *Warp* section of the Text Effects button Transform side menu.)
   d. Change the height of the WordArt to 4 inches and the width to 10 inches.
   e. Distribute the WordArt horizontally and vertically on the slide.
   f. Display the Format Background task pane. (Display this task pane by clicking the Format Background button on the DESIGN tab.) Insert a check mark in the *Hide background graphics* check box. Click the Preset gradients button, click the *Light Gradient - Accent 3* option (third column, first row), and then close the task pane.

4. Make Slide 4 active and then make the following changes:
   a. Select the bulleted text and then change the line spacing to double spacing (2.0). b. With the bulleted text selected, set the bulleted text in two columns. c. Size the placeholder so four bulleted items display in each column.

5. Make Slide 5 active and then insert the clip art image shown in Figure 4.20 with the following specifications: a. Use the words *watering can gardening tools* to search for the image. b. Flip the image horizontally. c. Change the height of the image to 4 inches. d. Display the Format Picture task pane with the Size & Properties icon selected and then change the horizontal position to 6 inches and the vertical position to 2.2 inches.

Celebrate Spring

think Spring!

June Magic

Preparing the Soil

1

P-C4-A2-GreenspacePres(A2).pptx (1 of 2)

Travel England (rotated layout):

10/23/2015

1. Open **TravelEngland.pptx** and then save the presentation with Save As and name it **P-C4-A1-TravelEngland**.
9. Apply the Peel Off transition to each slide.
12. Run the presentation.
13. Print the presentation as a handout with six slides printed horizontally per page.

3. Make Slide 2 active, select the text in the text box, and then set a left tab at the 0.5-inch mark, a center tab at the 6-inch mark, and a right tab at the 9.5-inch mark. Bold the headings in the first row.

Upcoming Tours

Dates	Duration	Price
April 17 through 24	8 days, 7 nights	$2499
May 15 through 22	8 days, 7 nights	$2495
June 12 through 19	8 days, 7 nights	$2599
July 8 through 18	11 days, 10 nights	$3099
July 24 through 31	8 days, 7 nights	$2599

Travel England

5. Make Slide 4 active and then insert the picture named **Stonehenge.jpg** located in the PC4 folder on your storage medium with the following specifications:
   a. Crop the picture so it displays as shown in Figure 4.14.
   b. Send the picture behind the text.
   c. Size and move the picture so it displays as shown in Figure 4.14.
   d. Size and move the bulleted text placeholder so it displays as shown in the figure.

Ancient Stone Circles
• Stonehenge
• Avebury
• The Sanctuary

Wilstshire
• Ancient stone circles
• Spectacular expansive views
• Gentle and pristine countryside
• History and heritage

4. Make Slide 6 active, select the picture, and then make the following changes:
   a. Use the Corrections button on the PICTURE TOOLS FORMAT tab to sharpen the image 25%.
   b. Display the Format Picture task pane with the Size & Properties icon selected.
   c. Change the scale height to 150%, the horizontal position to 5.5 inches, the vertical position to 2.2 inches, and then close the task pane.

White Horses
• Westbury
• Cherhill
• Pewsey
• Marlborough
• Alton Barnes
• Hackpen Hill
• Broad Town
• Devizes

Ancient Wiltshire
• Silbury Hill
• Knap Hill
• Woodhenge
• Amesbury
• Old Salisbury
• Savernake Forest

11. Insert a footer for notes and handouts pages that prints your first and last names.

10. Insert slide numbers on each slide.

1

Student Name

P-C4-A1-TravelEngland(A1).pptx

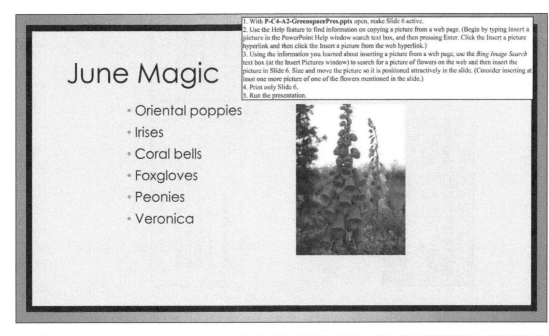

June Magic
- Oriental poppies
- Irises
- Coral bells
- Foxgloves
- Peonies
- Veronica

1. With **P-C4-A2-GreenspacePres.pptx** open, make Slide 6 active.
2. Use the Help feature to find information on copying a picture from a web page. (Begin by typing insert a picture in the PowerPoint Help window search text box, and then pressing Enter. Click the Insert a picture hyperlink and then click the Insert a picture from the web hyperlink.)
3. Using the information you learned about inserting a picture from a web page, use the *Bing Image Search* text box (at the Insert Pictures window) to search for a picture of flowers on the web and then insert the picture in Slide 6. Size and move the picture so it is positioned attractively in the slide. (Consider inserting at least one more picture of one of the flowers mentioned in the slide.)
4. Print only Slide 6.
5. Run the presentation.

P-C4-A2-GreenspacePres(A3,Slide6).pptx

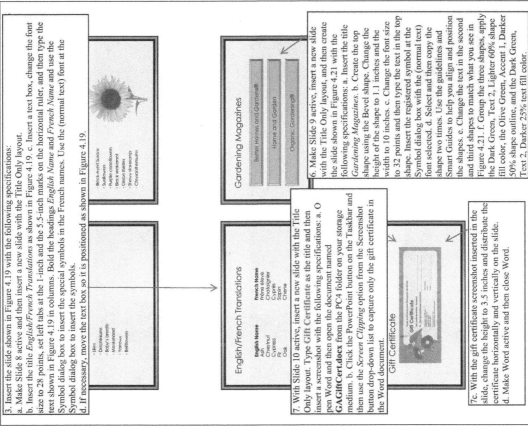

3. Insert the slide shown in Figure 4.19 with the following specifications:
a. Make Slide 8 active and then insert a new slide with the Title Only layout.
b. Insert the title *English/French Translations* as shown in Figure 4.19. c. Insert a text box, change the font size to 28 points, set left tabs at the 1-inch and the 5.5-inch marks on the horizontal ruler, and then type the text shown in Figure 4.19 in columns. Bold the headings *English Name* and *French Name* and use the Symbol dialog box to insert the special symbols in the French names. Use the (normal text) font at the Symbol dialog box to insert the symbols.
d. If necessary, move the text box so it is positioned as shown in Figure 4.19.

6. Make Slide 9 active, insert a new slide with the Title Only layout, and then create the slide shown in Figure 4.21 with the following specifications: a. Insert the title *Gardening Magazines*. b. Create the top shape using the Bevel shape. Change the height of the shape to 1.1 inches and the width to 10 inches. c. Change the font size to 32 points and then type the text in the top shape. Insert the registered symbol at the Symbol dialog box with the (normal text) font selected. d. Select and then copy the shape two times. Use the guidelines and Smart Guides to help you align and position the shapes. e. Change the text in the second and third shapes to match what you see in Figure 4.21. f. Group the three shapes, apply the Dark Green, Text 2, Lighter 60% shape fill color, the Olive Green, Accent 1, Darker 50% shape outline, and the Dark Green, Text 2, Darker 25% text fill color.

7. With Slide 10 active, insert a new slide with the Title Only layout. Type Gift Certificate as the title and then insert a screenshot with the following specifications: a. O pen Word and then open the document named **GAGiftCert.docx** from the PC4 folder on your storage medium. b. Click the PowerPoint button on the Taskbar and then use the *Screen Clipping* option from the Screenshot button drop-down list to capture only the gift certificate in the Word document.

7c. With the gift certificate screenshot inserted in the slide, change the height to 3.5 inches and distribute the certificate horizontally and vertically on the slide.
d. Make Word active and then close Word.

P-C4-A2-GreenspacePres(A2).pptx (2 of 2)

BUDGETING

HONORÉ FINANCIAL SERVICES
Managing Your Money

Successful Budgeting:
- Establish a budget.
- Live within the budget.
- Spend less money than you make.
- Start a saving and investment plan.

Gathering Information:
- Determine your average monthly income.
- Determine your monthly fixed expenses.
- Determine your monthly variable expenses.
- Evaluate your expenses.
- Track all of your expenses by keeping receipts.
- Set goals and objectives.

P-C4-CS-HFS(CS1).pptx (1 of 2)

Study Rome!

Study Abroad
Rome, Italy

Courses

Accommodations

Contact Information

P-C4-VB-RomeStudy(VB).pptx

P-C4-CS-HFS(CS2,Slide8).pptx

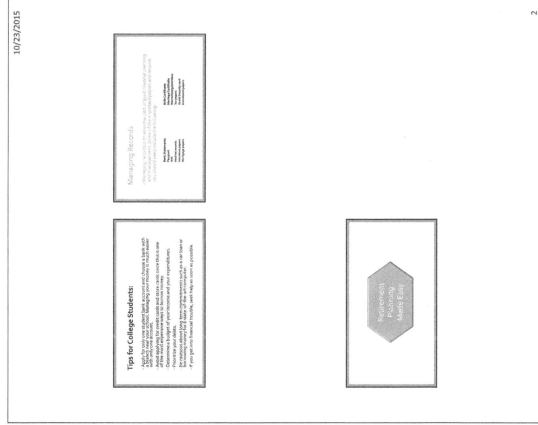

P-C4-CS-HFS(CS1).pptx (2 of 2)

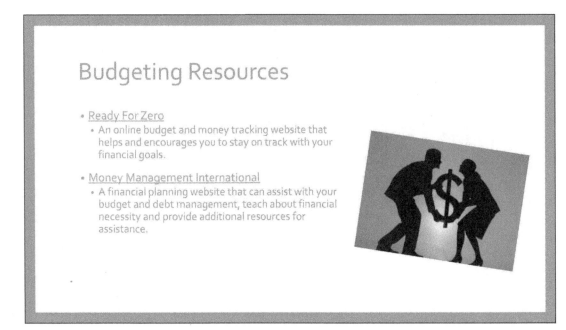

P-C4-CS-HFS(CS4,Slide9).pptx

P-C4-CS-HFSWorkshop(CS3).pptx

PowerPoint Performance Assessment Unit 1 Model Answers

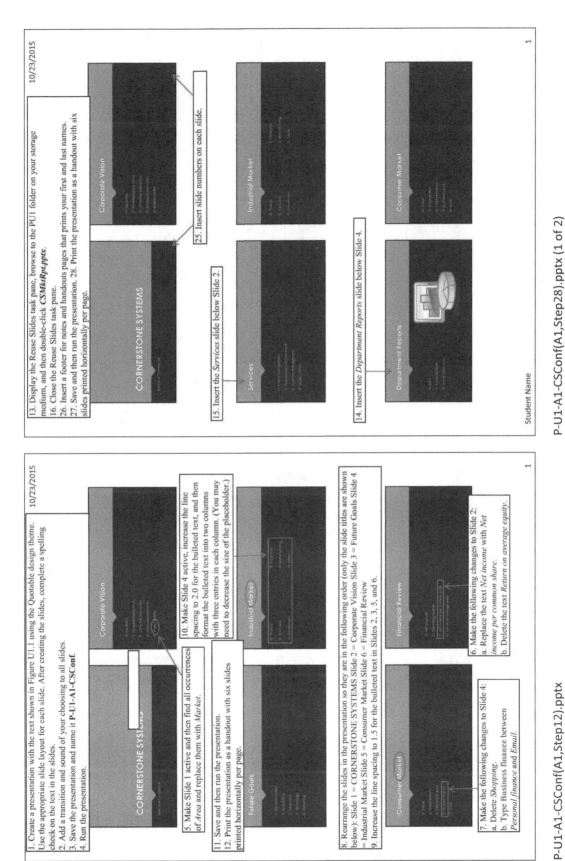

10/23/2015

Corporate Vision

CORNERSTONE SYSTEMS

25. Insert slide numbers on each slide.

Industrial Market

15. Insert the *Services* slide below Slide 2.

Services

Consumer Market

14. Insert the *Department Reports* slide below Slide 4.

Department Reports

13. Display the Reuse Slides task pane, browse to the PU1 folder on your storage medium, and then double-click *CSMktRpt.pptx*.
16. Close the Reuse Slides task pane.
26. Insert a footer for notes and handouts pages that prints your first and last names.
27. Save and then run the presentation. 28. Print the presentation as a handout with six slides printed horizontally per page.

Student Name

P-U1-A1-CSConf(A1,Step28).pptx (1 of 2)

10/23/2015

Corporate Vision

CORNERSTONE SYSTEMS

5. Make Slide 1 active and then find all occurrences of *Area* and replace them with *Market*.

Industrial Market

10. Make Slide 4 active, increase the line spacing to 2.0 for the bulleted text, and then format the bulleted text into two columns with three entries in each column. (You may need to decrease the size of the placeholder.)

Future Goals

11. Save and then run the presentation.
12. Print the presentation as a handout with six slides printed horizontally per page.

Consumer Market

7. Make the following changes to Slide 4:
a. Delete *Shopping*.
b. Type Business finance between *Personal finance* and *Email*.

Financial Review

8. Rearrange the slides in the presentation so they are in the following order (only the slide titles are shown below): Slide 1 = CORNERSTONE SYSTEMS Slide 2 = Corporate Vision Slide 3 = Future Goals Slide 4 = Industrial Market Slide 5 = Consumer Market Slide 6 = Financial Review
9. Increase the line spacing to 1.5 for the bulleted text in Slides 2, 3, 5, and 6.

6. Make the following changes to Slide 2:
a. Replace the text *Net income* with *Net income per common share*.
b. Delete the text *Return on average equity*.

1. Create a presentation with the text shown in Figure U1.1 using the Quotable design theme. Use the appropriate slide layout for each slide. After creating the slides, complete a spelling check on the text in the slides.
2. Add a transition and sound of your choosing to all slides.
3. Save the presentation and name it **P-U1-A1-CSConf**.
4. Run the presentation.

P-U1-A1-CSConf(A1,Step12).pptx

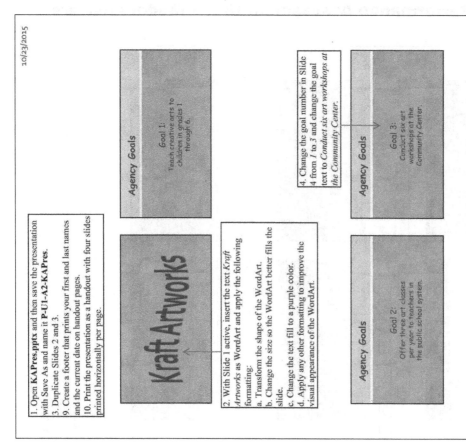

1. Open **KAPres.pptx** and then save the presentation with Save As and name it **P-U1-A2-KAPres**.
3. Duplicate Slides 2 and 3.
9. Create a footer that prints your first and last names and the current date on handout pages.
10. Print the presentation as a handout with four slides printed horizontally per page.

2. With Slide 1 active, insert the text *Kraft Artworks* as WordArt and apply the following formatting:
a. Transform the shape of the WordArt.
b. Change the size so the WordArt better fills the slide.
c. Change the text fill to a purple color.
d. Apply any other formatting to improve the visual appearance of the WordArt.

4. Change the goal number in Slide 4 from *1* to *3* and change the goal text to *Conduct six art workshops at the Community Center.*

Agency Goals
Goal 1:
Teach creative arts to children in grades 1 through 6.

Kraft Artworks

Agency Goals
Goal 2:
Offer three art classes per year to teachers in the public school system.

Agency Goals
Goal 3:
Conduct six art workshops of the Community Center.

Student Name

P-U1-A2-KAPres(A2).pptx (1 of 2)

---

17. Make Slide 8 active, select the bulleted text, and then create and apply a custom bullet using a dollar sign in a complementary color and set the size to 100%. (You can find a dollar sign in the normal text font in the Symbol dialog box.)

19. Move Slide 4 (*Future Goals*) to the end of the presentation.
21. Make Slide 8 active, select the bulleted items, and then apply numbering.

18. With Slide 8 active, insert a clip art image related to money or finances. Format, size, and then position the clip art attractively on the slide.

20. Insert a new slide with the Title and Content layout at the end of the presentation with the following specifications:
a. Insert *Future Goals* as the title. b. Type *International market* as the first bulleted item and then press Enter. c. Copy *Acquisitions, Production, Technology,* and *Marketing* from Slide 8 and paste them in the content area of the new slide below the first line of bulleted text. (When copied, the items should be preceded by a bullet. If a bullet displays on a blank line below the last text item, press the Backspace key twice.) d. Select the bulleted text and then change the line spacing to 1.5.

22. Make Slide 9 active, select the bulleted items, apply numbering, and then change the beginning number to *6*.

23. With Slide 9 active, create a new slide with the Blank layout with the following specifications: a. Insert **Nightscape.jpg** as a background picture and hide the background graphics. *Hint: Do this with the Format Background button on the DESIGN tab.* b. Create a text box toward the top of the slide, change the font color to White, Text 1, increase the font size to 36 points, and then change the alignment to center. c. Type National Sales Meeting, press Enter, type New York City, press Enter, and then type March 4 to 6, 2015. d. Move and/or size the text box so the text is positioned centered above the buildings in the picture.

24. With Slide 10 active, insert a new slide with the Title Only layout. Type Doubletree Guest Suites as the title and then insert a screenshot with the following specifications: a. Open Word and then open **HotelMap.docx** from the PU1 folder on your storage medium. b. Click the PowerPoint button on the Taskbar and then use the *Screen Clipping* option from the Screenshot button drop-down list to capture only the map in the Word document. c. With the map screenshot inserted in the slide, apply the Sharpen: 25% correction. Size and position the map attractively on the slide.

Financial Review

Future Goals

National Sales Meeting
New York City
March 4 to 6, 2015

Future Goals

Doubletree Guest Suites

Student Name

P-U1-A1-CSConf(A1,Step28).pptx (2 of 2)

10/23/2015

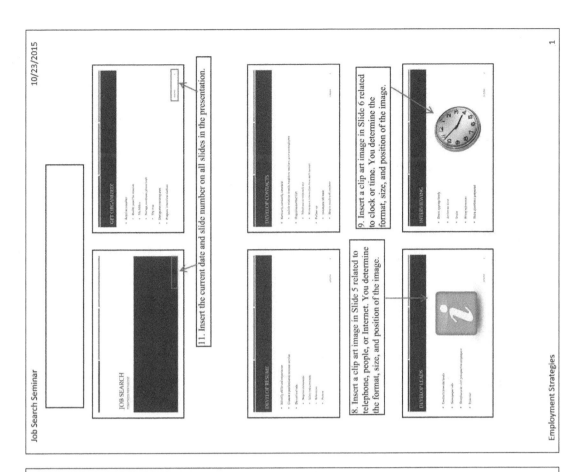

11. Insert the current date and slide number on all slides in the presentation.

9. Insert a clip art image in Slide 6 related to clock or time. You determine the format, size, and position of the image.

8. Insert a clip art image in Slide 5 related to telephone, people, or Internet. You determine the format, size, and position of the image.

Employment Strategies

P-U1-A3-JobSearch(A3,Step16).pptx (1 of 2)

1

10/23/2015

6. With Slide 5 active, insert a new slide with the Title Only layout with the following specifications: a. Insert the title *Clients* and then format, size, and position the title in the same manner as the title in Slide 5. b. Insert a text box, change the font to Comic Sans MS and the font size to 20 points, apply the Lavender, Accent 1, Darker 50% font color and then type the following text in columns (you determine the tab settings): **School Contact Number** Logan Elementary School Maya Jones 555-0882 Cedar Elementary School George Ferraro 555-3211 Sunrise Elementary School Avery Burns 555-3444 Hillside Middle School Joanna Myers 555-2211 Douglas Middle School Ray Murphy 555-8100 c. Select all of the text in the text box and then change the line spacing to 1.5.

5. Change the goal number in Slide 5 from *2* to *4* and change the goal text to *Provide recycled material to public schools for art classes.*

Agency Goals

Goal 4: Provide recycled material to public schools for art classes.

Clients

8. With Slide 7 active, insert a new slide with the Blank layout, hide the background graphic, and then create the slide shown in Figure U1.3 with the following specifications: a. Set the text in the two text boxes at the left and right sides of the slide in 54-point Comic Sans MS with bold formatting and in the Lavender, Accent 1, Darker 50% font color. Rotate, size, and position the two text boxes as shown in Figure U1.3. b. Use the Explosion 1 shape to create the shape in the middle of the slide. c. Apply the Light Green shape fill color, the Lavender, 18 pt glow, Accent color 2 glow effect, the Perspective Diagonal Upper Left shadow effect, the Lavender, Accent 1, Darker 50% shape outline color, and the 2¼ points shape outline weight. d. Insert the text in the shape and then change the font to 28-point Comic Sans MS, apply bold formatting, and then apply the Lavender, Accent 1, Darker 50% font color. Change the alignments to *Center* and change the vertical alignment to *Middle*.

Kraft Artworks

Kraft Artworks

Supporting and encouraging creativity!

KIDS!

ART

FUN!

7. With Slide 6 active, insert a new slide with the Blank layout, hide the background graphic, and then create the slide shown in Figure U1.2 with the following specifications: a. Use the Explosion 1 shape (in the *Stars and Banners* section) to create the first shape. b. Apply the Light Green shape fill color and apply the Lavender, 18 pt glow, Accent color 2 glow effect. c. With the shape selected, change the font to 40-point Comic Sans MS with bold formatting and in the Lavender, Accent 1, Darker 50% font color and then type the text shown in Figure U1.2. d. Copy the shape twice and position the shapes as shown in Figure U1.2. e. Type the appropriate text in each shape as shown in Figure U1.2.

Student Name

P-U1-A2-KAPres(A2).pptx (2 of 2)

2

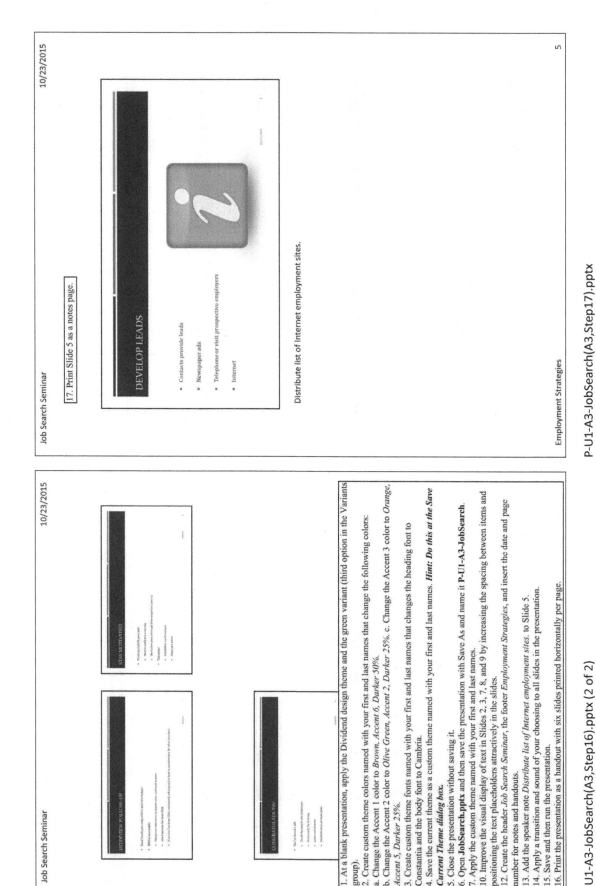

17. Print Slide 5 as a notes page.

DEVELOP LEADS

- Contacts provide leads
- Newspaper ads
- Telephone or visit prospective employers
- Internet

Distribute list of Internet employment sites.

Employment Strategies

P-U1-A3-JobSearch(A3,Step17).pptx

5

Job Search Seminar

10/23/2015

STAY MOTIVATED

INTERVIEW FOLLOW-UP

CONGRATULATIONS!

1. At a blank presentation, apply the Dividend design theme and the green variant (third option in the Variants group).
2. Create custom theme colors named with your first and last names that change the following colors:
a. Change the Accent 1 color to *Brown, Accent 6, Darker 50%*.
b. Change the Accent 2 color to *Olive Green, Accent 2, Darker 25%*. c. Change the Accent 3 color to *Orange, Accent 5, Darker 25%*.
3. Create custom theme fonts named with your first and last names that changes the heading font to Constantia and the body font to Cambria.
4. Save the current theme as a custom theme named with your first and last names. ***Hint: Do this at the Save Current Theme dialog box.***
5. Close the presentation without saving it.
6. Open **JobSearch.pptx** and then save the presentation with Save As and name it **P-U1-A3-JobSearch**.
7. Apply the custom theme named with your first and last names.
10. Improve the visual display of text in Slides 2, 3, 7, 8, and 9 by increasing the spacing between items and positioning the text placeholders attractively in the slides.
12. Create the header *Job Search Seminar*, the footer *Employment Strategies*, and insert the date and page number for notes and handouts.
13. Add the speaker note *Distribute list of Internet employment sites.* to Slide 5.
14. Apply a transition and sound of your choosing to all slides in the presentation.
15. Save and then run the presentation.
16. Print the presentation as a handout with six slides printed horizontally per page.

P-U1-A3-JobSearch(A3,Step16).pptx (2 of 2)

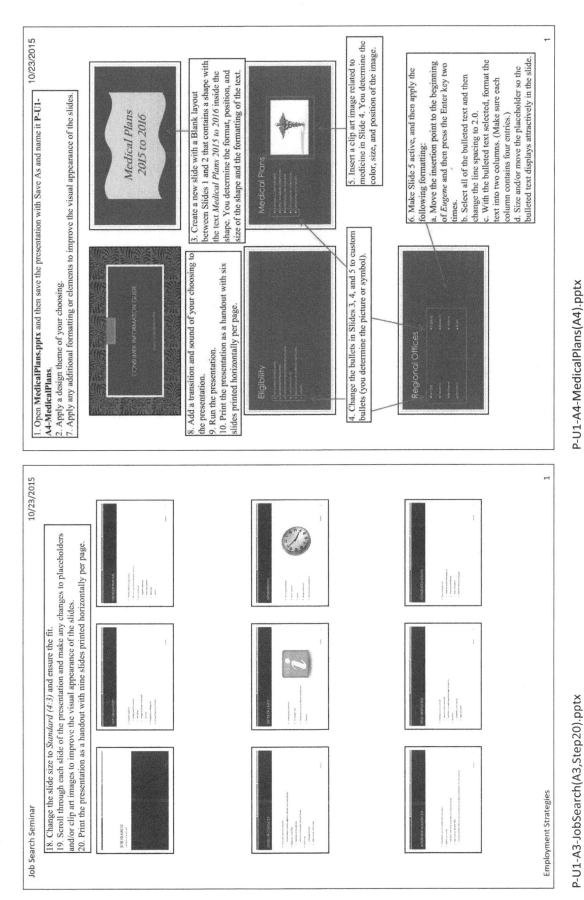

10/23/2015

1. Open **MedicalPlans.pptx** and then save the presentation with Save As and name it **P-U1-A4-MedicalPlans**.
2. Apply a design theme of your choosing.
7. Apply any additional formatting or elements to improve the visual appearance of the slides.

3. Create a new slide with a Blank layout between Slides 1 and 2 that contains a shape with the text *Medical Plans 2015 to 2016* inside the shape. You determine the format, position, and size of the shape and the formatting of the text.

5. Insert a clip art image related to medicine in Slide 4. You determine the color, size, and position of the image.

6. Make Slide 5 active, and then apply the following formatting:
a. Move the insertion point to the beginning of *Eugene* and then press the Enter key two times.
b. Select all of the bulleted text and then change the line spacing to 2.0.
c. With the bulleted text selected, format the text into two columns. (Make sure each column contains four entries.)
d. Size and/or move the placeholder so the bulleted text displays attractively in the slide.

8. Add a transition and sound of your choosing to the presentation.
9. Run the presentation.
10. Print the presentation as a handout with six slides printed horizontally per page.

4. Change the bullets in Slides 3, 4, and 5 to custom bullets (you determine the picture or symbol).

P-U1-A4-MedicalPlans(A4).pptx

10/23/2015

Job Search Seminar

18. Change the slide size to *Standard (4:3)* and ensure the fit.
19. Scroll through each slide of the presentation and make any changes to placeholders and/or clip art images to improve the visual appearance of the slides.
20. Print the presentation as a handout with nine slides printed horizontally per page.

Employment Strategies

P-U1-A3-JobSearch(A3,Step20).pptx

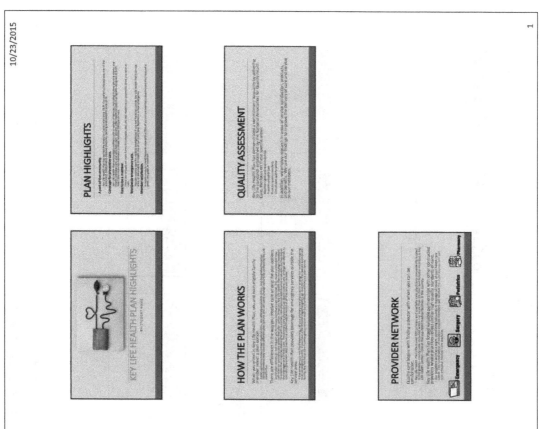

P-U1-Act2-JPGPres.pptx

P-U1-Act1-KLHPlan.pptx

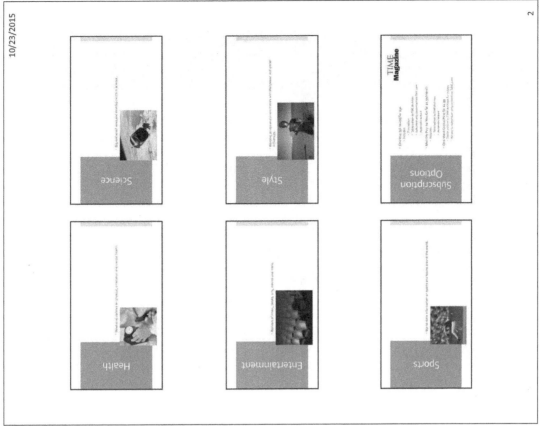

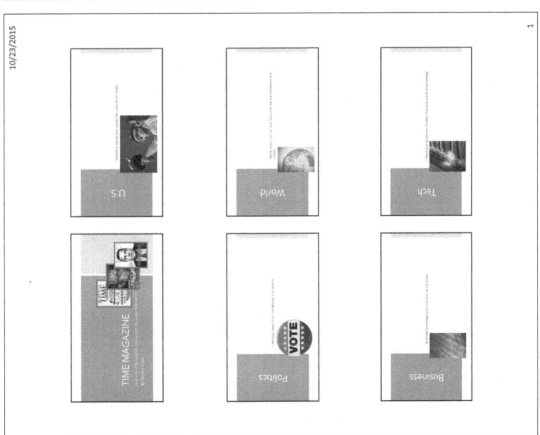

PowerPoint Chapter 5 Model Answers

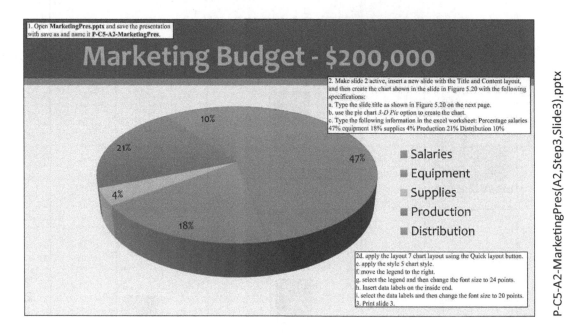

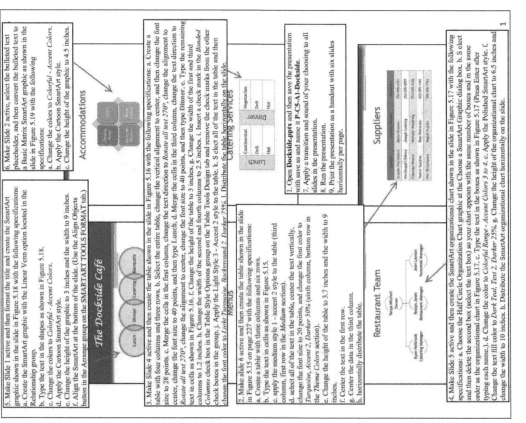

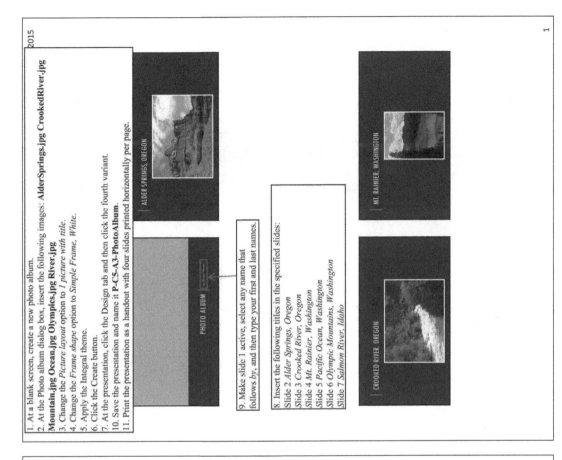

Top slide panel — P-C5-A3-PhotoAlbum(A3).pptx (1 of 2)

1. At a blank screen, create a new photo album.
2. At the Photo album dialog box, insert the following images: **AlderSprings.jpg CrookedRiver.jpg Mountain.jpg Ocean.jpg Olympics.jpg River.jpg**
3. Change the *Picture layout* option to *1 picture with title*.
4. Change the *Frame shape* option to *Simple Frame, White*.
5. Apply the Integral theme.
6. Click the Create button.
7. At the presentation, click the Design tab and then click the fourth variant.
8. Insert the following titles in the specified slides:
Slide 2 *Alder Springs, Oregon*
Slide 3 *Crooked River, Oregon*
Slide 4 *Mt. Rainier, Washington*
Slide 5 *Pacific Ocean, Washington*
Slide 6 *Olympic Mountains, Washington*
Slide 7 *Salmon River, Idaho*
9. Make slide 1 active, select any name that follows *by*, and then type your first and last names.
10. Save the presentation and name it **P-C5-A3-PhotoAlbum**.
11. Print the presentation as a handout with four slides printed horizontally per page.

Bottom slide panel — P-C5-A2-MarketingPres(A2,Step8).pptx

4. After looking at the slide, you realize that two of the percentages are incorrect. Edit the Excel data and change 47% to 42% and change *10% to 15%*.
6. Apply a transition and sound of your choosing to each slide in the presentation.
7. Run the presentation.
8. Print the presentation as a handout with six slides printed horizontally per page.
5. With slide 3 active, insert a new slide with the Title and Content layout and then create the chart shown in the slide in Figure 5.21 with the following specifications:
a. Type the slide title as shown in Figure 5.21.
b. use the line chart *Line with Markers* option to create the chart.
c. Type the following information in the excel worksheet: revenues expenses 1st Qtr $789,560 $670,500 2nd Qtr $990,450 $765,000 3rd Qtr $750,340 $780,000 4th Qtr $980,400 $875,200
d. Apply the style 4 chart style.
e. Add primary major vertical gridlines.
5f. Add a data table with legend keys.
g. Remove the title and remove the legend.
h. Select the chart area and then change the font size to 18 points.
i. With the chart area still selected, display the Format Chart area task pane and then specify a gradient fill of *Light Gradient - Accent 2*.
j. Select the revenues series and then change the weight of the line to 4 ½ points. (Do this with the shape outline button in the shape styles group on the Chart Tools Format tab.)
k. Select the expenses series and then change the weight of the line to 4 ½ points.

P-C5-A3-PhotoAlbum(A3).pptx (1 of 2)

P-C5-A2-MarketingPres(A2,Step8).pptx

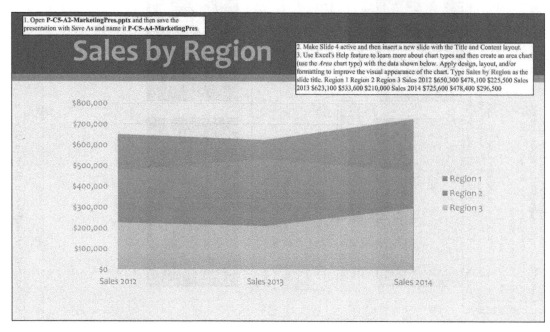

P-C5-A4-MarketingPres(A4).pptx

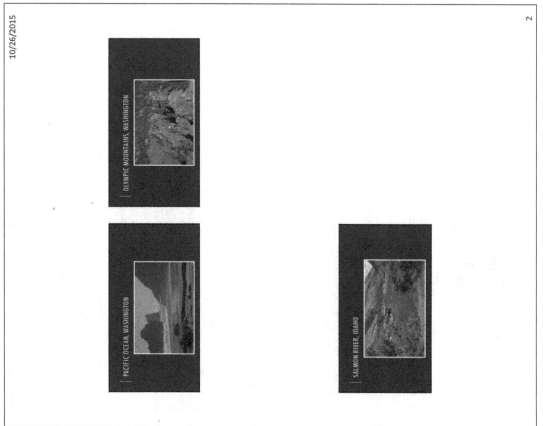

10/26/2015

2

P-C5-A3-PhotoAlbum(A3).pptx (2 of 2)

Benchmark PowerPoint 2013 Model Answers

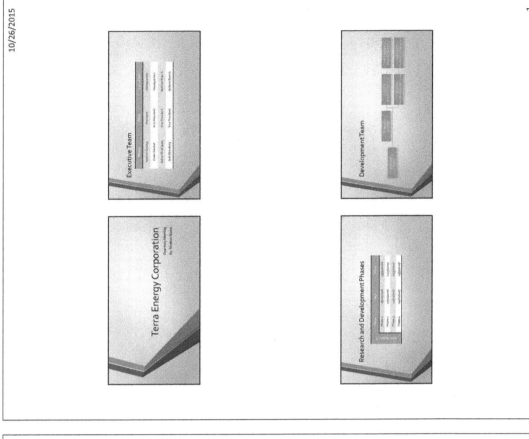

10/26/2015

P-C5-CS-TECPres(CS1).pptx (1 of 2)

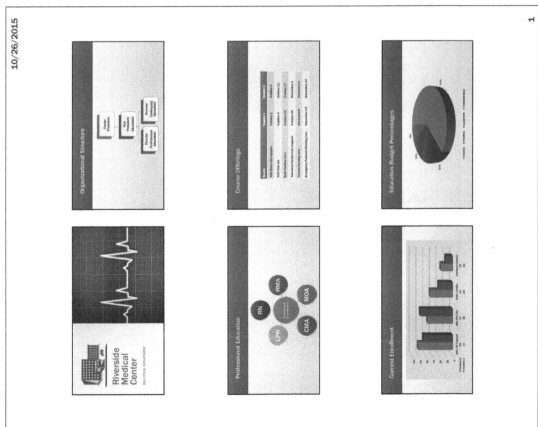

10/26/2015

P-C5-VB-RMCPres(VB).pptx

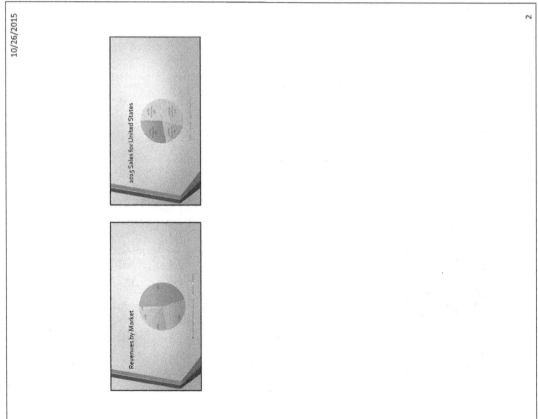

P-C5-CS-TECPres(CS2).pptx (1 of 2)

P-C5-CS-TECPres(CS1).pptx (2 of 2)

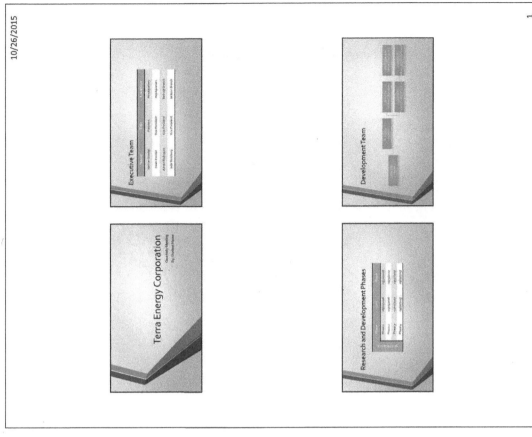

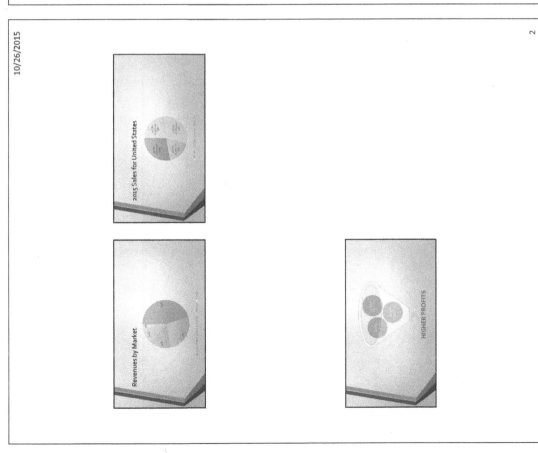

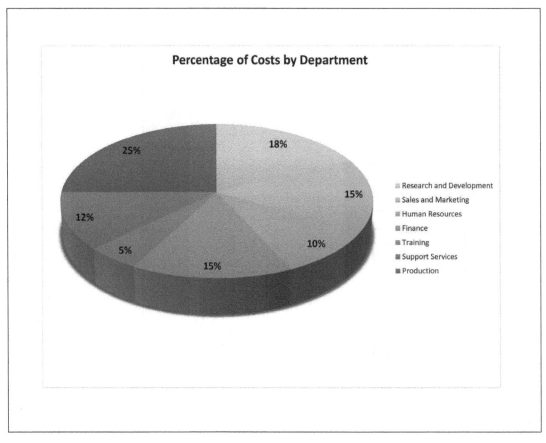

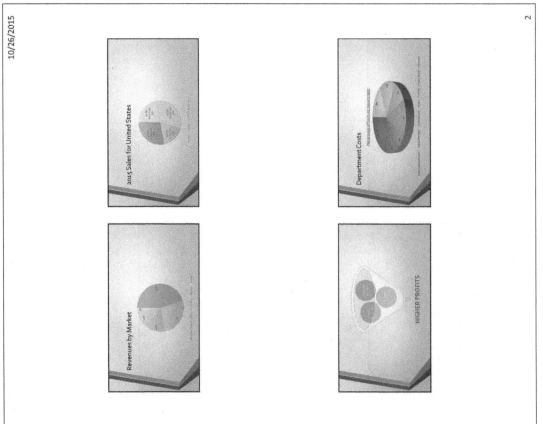

PowerPoint Chapter 6 Model Answers

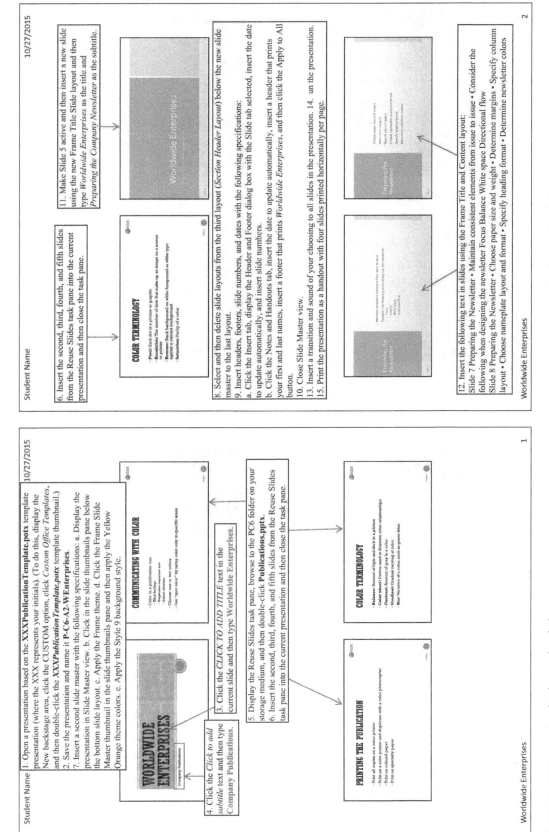

Top section (page 2):

10/27/2015

7. Make sure you are connected to the Internet and then run the presentation beginning with Slide 1. Navigate through the slide show by clicking the next action button and display the connected presentation by clicking the clip art image in Slide 2. At Slide 8, click the Organic Gardening® hyperlink. Scroll through the website and click a few different hyperlinks that interest you. After viewing a few web pages in the magazine, close your web browser. When you click the action button on the last slide, the first slide displays. End the slide show by pressing the Esc key.

8. Print the presentation as a handout with four slides printed horizontally per page.

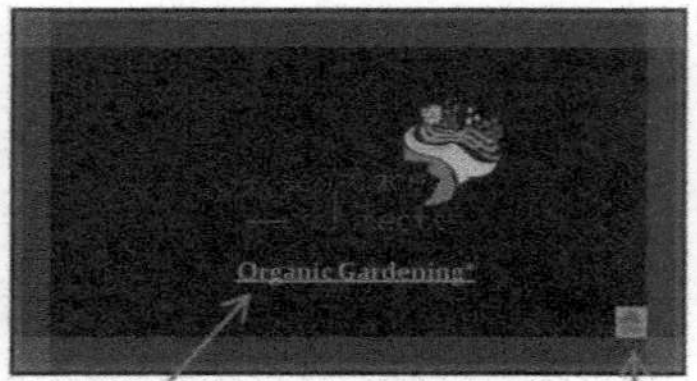

6. Display Slide 8 active and then make the following changes:
a. Delete the text *Better Homes and Gardens*® and then type *Organic Gardening*®.
b. Select *Organic Gardening*® and then create a hyperlink with the text to the website www.organicgardening.com.

4. Make Slide 8 active and then create an action button that displays the first slide in the presentation.

Bottom section (page 1):

10/27/2015

1. Open **GAPres.pptx** and then save the presentation with the name **P-C6-A3-GAPres**.
3. Display the presentation in Slide Master view, click the top slide master in the slide thumbnails pane, create an action button in the lower right corner of the slide that displays the next slide, and then close Slide Master view.

5. Make Slide 2 active, click the flowers clip art image, and then create a link to the presentation **MaintenancePres.pptx** (located in the PC6 folder on your storage medium). *Hint: Use the Action button in the Links group on the Insert tab.*

2. Make Slide 1 active and then insert an action button in the lower right corner of the slide that displays the next slide.

Statistics

* Location: Pinellas County, Florida
* Land area: 5.5 square miles
* Average condo value: $174,000
* Average home value: $265,367
* Active businesses: 1,844
* Cumulative payroll: $895,644,000

Worldwide Enterprises

Presented Branch Office
Clearwater, Florida

Population

* Estimated population: 107,685
* Female: 52.1%
* Male: 47.9%
* Median age: 43.8 years
* Median household income: $39,849
* Unemployed: 6.6%

Distribution of imputed household income (numbers of persons)

Health Care

* 15 clinics and ambulatory care centers
* 50 hospitals
* 9,200+ physicians
* 58,000+ nurses

Top Public Employers

* Pinellas County School District
* Pinellas County Government
* Pinellas County Sheriff's Department
* Bay Pines VA Medical Center

Action Buttons

LEARNING AND USING DIFFERENT ACTION BUTTON FEATURES

Back or Previous

This button lets you move backwards through your presentation, one slide at a time.

Forward or Next

This button will move you forward through your presentation.

Beginning of Presentation

This button will quickly move you to the beginning of your presentation.

End of Presentation

This button quickly moves you to the end of your presentation.

1. In this chapter, you learned to insert a number of action buttons in a slide. Experiment with the other action buttons (click the Insert tab, click the Shapes button, and then point to the buttons in the *Action Buttons* section) and then prepare a PowerPoint presentation with the following specifications:
a. The first slide should contain the title of your presentation.
b. Choose four action buttons and then create one slide for each of the action buttons that includes the specific name as well as an explanation of the button.
c. Apply a design theme of your choosing to the presentation.
2. Save the presentation and name it **P-C6-A4-ActionButtons**.
3. Print the presentation as a handout with six slides printed horizontally per page.

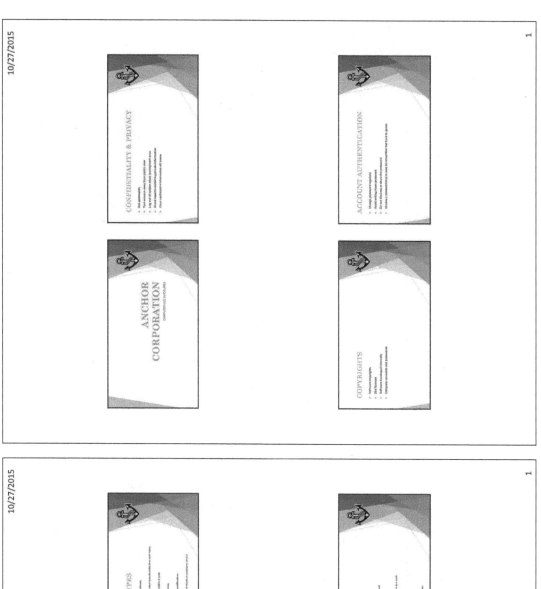

P-C6-CS-AnchorGuidelines(CS3).pptx (1 of 2)

P-C6-CS-AnchorEmp(CS2).pptx

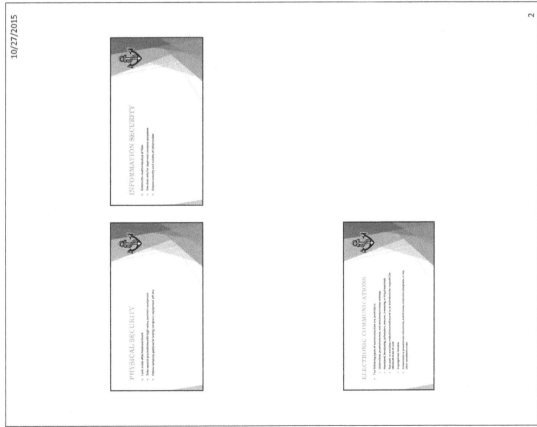

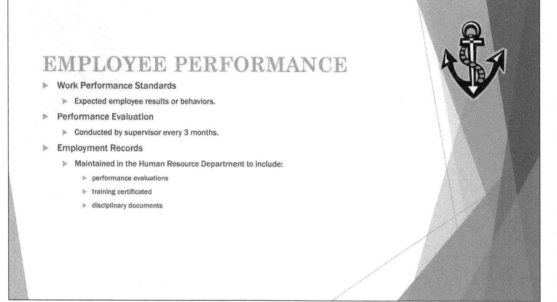

EMPLOYEE PERFORMANCE

- ▶ Work Performance Standards
  - ▶ Expected employee results or behaviors.
- ▶ Performance Evaluation
  - ▶ Conducted by supervisor every 3 months.
- ▶ Employment Records
  - ▶ Maintained in the Human Resource Department to include:
    - ▶ performance evaluations
    - ▶ training certificated
    - ▶ disciplinary documents

APPOINTMENT TYPES

- ▶ New Hire
  - ▶ on acceptance of appointment, 6 month probationary
- ▶ Reemployment
  - ▶ military, laid off, reclassification, seasons, and short term disability from work injury
- ▶ Reinstatement
  - ▶ resigned employees reinstated to similar class within 2 years
- ▶ Reappointment
  - ▶ to former position if meets minimum qualifications
- ▶ Demotion
  - ▶ request or accept a lower grade level if meets qualifications
- ▶ Promotion
  - ▶ compete for promotional openings after initial 6 month of continuous service

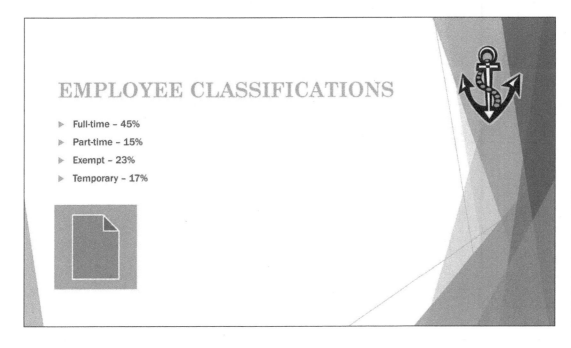

EMPLOYEE CLASSIFICATIONS

- Full-time – 45%
- Part-time – 15%
- Exempt – 23%
- Temporary – 17%

COMPENSATION

- Rate of Pay
  - each grade contains 10 steps
- Direct Deposit Option
  - forward payment to a savings or checking account
- Pay Progression
  - annual merit salary increases
- Overtime
  - exceeds 8hrs a day, 8hrs in 16hr period, or 40hrs in a week
- Longevity Pay
  - awarded after 8 years of continuous service
- Payment for Holidays
  - paid status for 11 holidays per year
- Shift Differential
  - adjustment of additional 5% of normal rate of pay

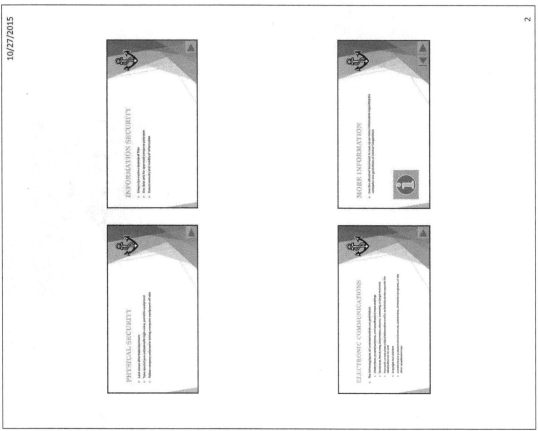

P-C6-CS-AnchorGuidelines(CS5).pptx (2 of 2)

P-C6-CS-AnchorGuidelines(CS5).pptx (1 of 2)

Benchmark PowerPoint 2013 Model Answers

PowerPoint Chapter 7 Model Answers

1. Open **JobSearch.pptx** and then save the presentation with Save As and name it **P-C7-A3-JobSearch**.
2. Apply the Wisp design theme and the blue-colored variant (third thumbnail) to the presentation.
3. Add appropriate clip art images to at least two slides.
4. Make Slide 10 active and then insert the video file named **Flight.mov** from the PC7 folder on your storage medium. Make the following changes to the video:
   a. Click the Video Tools Format tab and then change the height to 5 inches.
   b. Distribute the video horizontally on the slide.
   c. Click the Video Tools Playback tab and then specify that you want the video to play automatically (do this with the *Start* option box), that you want the video to play full screen, and that you want the video to hide while not playing.
   d. Click the Trim Video button and then trim approximately the first nine seconds from the start of the video. Click OK to close the dialog box.
5. With Slide 10 active, insert the **AudioFile-03.mid** audio file in the slide (located in the PC7 folder on your storage medium) so it plays automatically, loops until stopped, and is hidden when running the presentation.
6. Compress the video file for Internet quality.
7. Run the presentation. After listening to the music for a period of time, end the presentation.
8. Print only Slide 10.

P-C7-A3-JobSearch(A3,Step8,Slide10).pptx

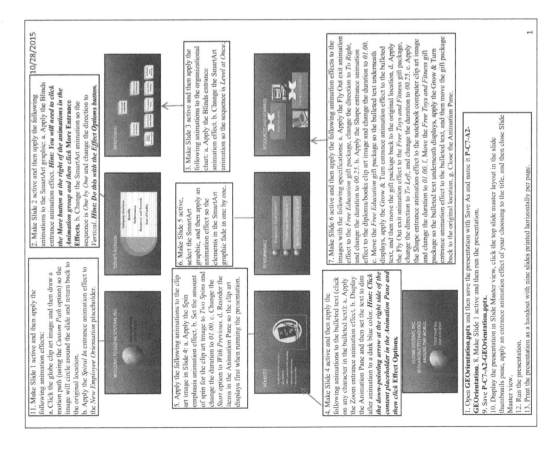

P-C7-A2-GEOrientation(A2).pptx

10/28/2015

12. Edit the Interview custom show by removing Slide 2.
13. Print the Interview custom show again as a handout with all slides printed horizontally on one page.

JOB SEARCH

Interviewing

Interview Follow-Up

Congratulations!

P-C7-A3-JobSearch(A3,Step13).pptx

10/28/2015

9. Create a custom show named *Interview* that contains Slides 1, 3, 6, 7, and 9. 10. Run the Interview custom show.
11. Print the Interview custom show as a handout with all slides printed horizontally on one page.

JOB SEARCH

Develop Resume

Interviewing

Interview Follow-Up

Congratulations!

P-C7-A3-JobSearch(A3,Step11).pptx

Benchmark PowerPoint 2013 Model Answers

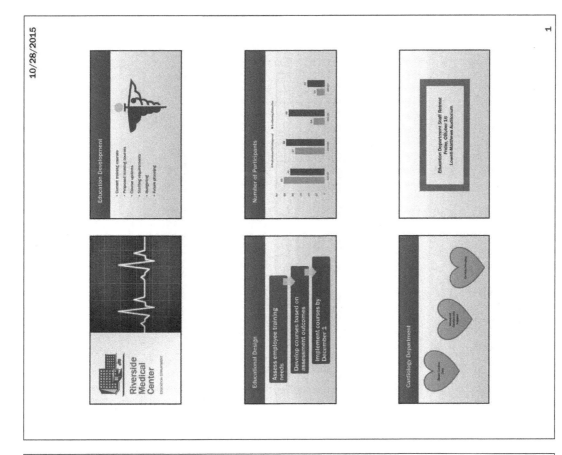

P-C7-VB-RMCPres(VB).pptx

P-C7-A4-JamaicaTour(A4).pptx

P-C7-CS-PCBuyGuide(CS1).pptx (2 of 3)

P-C7-CS-PCBuyGuide(CS1).pptx (1 of 3)

Benchmark PowerPoint 2013 Model Answers

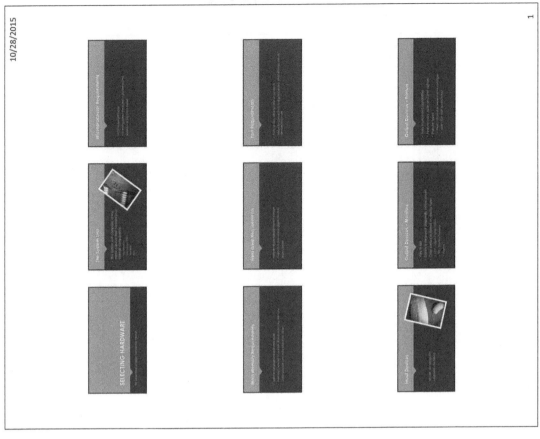

P-C7-CS-PCBuyGuide(CS2).pptx

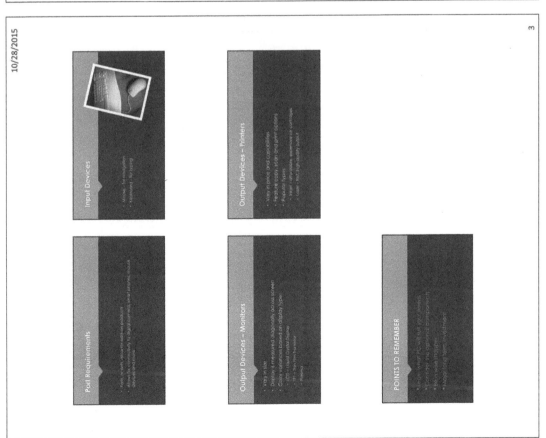

P-C7-CS-PCBuyGuide(CS1).pptx (3 of 3)

PowerPoint Chapter 8 Model Answers

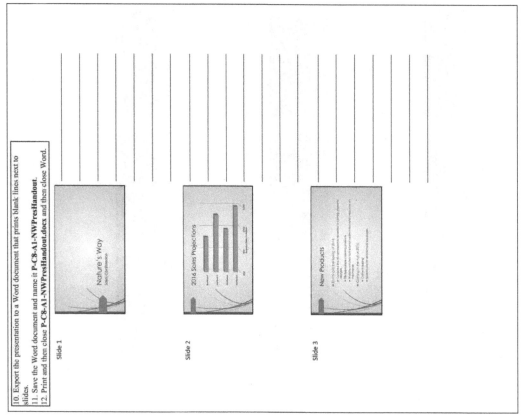

10. Export the presentation to a Word document that prints blank lines next to slides.
11. Save the Word document and name it **P-C8-A1-NWPresHandout.docx**.
12. Print and then close **P-C8-A1-NWPresHandout.docx** and then close Word.

Slide 1

Slide 2

Slide 3

P-C8-A1-NWPresHandout(A1).pptx (1 of 2)

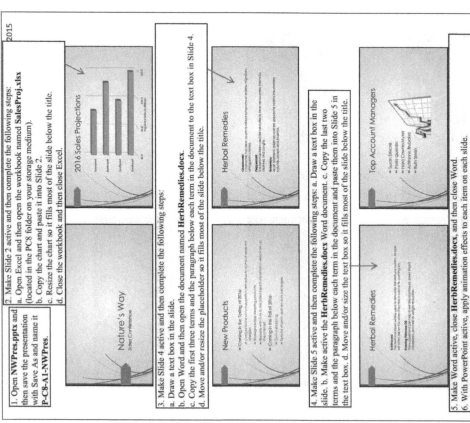

1. Open **NWPres.pptx** and then save the presentation with Save As and name it **P-C8-A1-NWPres**.

2. Make Slide 2 active and then complete the following steps:
   a. Open Excel and then open the workbook named **SalesProj.xlsx** (located in the PC8 folder on your storage medium).
   b. Copy the chart and paste it into Slide 2.
   c. Resize the chart so it fills most of the slide below the title.
   d. Close the workbook and then close Excel.

3. Make Slide 4 active and then complete the following steps:
   a. Draw a text box in the slide.
   b. Open Word and then open the document named **HerbRemedies.docx**.
   c. Copy the first three terms and the paragraph below each term in the document to the text box in Slide 4.
   d. Move and/or resize the placeholder so it fills most of the slide below the title.

4. Make Slide 5 active and then complete the following steps: a. Draw a text box in the slide. b. Make active the **HerbRemedies.docx** Word document. c. Copy the last two terms and the paragraph below each term in the document and paste them into Slide 5 in the text box. d. Move and/or size the text box so it fills most of the slide below the title.

5. Make Word active, close **HerbRemedies.docx**, and then close Word.
6. With PowerPoint active, apply animation effects to each item on each slide.
7. Run the presentation.
8. Save **P-C8-A1-NWPres.pptx**.
9. Print the presentation as a handout with six slides printed horizontally per page.

P-C8-A1-NWPres(A1).pptx

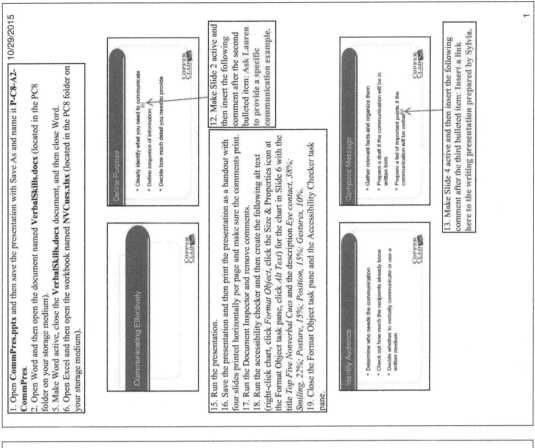

P-C8-A2-CommPres(A2,Step16).pptx (1 of 2)

P-C8-A1-NWPresHandout(A1).pptx (2 of 2)

6. Open **P-C8-A1-NWPres.pptx** and then save the presentation in PDF file format. When the presentation displays in Adobe Reader, scroll through the presentation and then close Adobe Reader.

7. In PowerPoint, close **P-C8-A1-NWPres.pptx**.

Nature's Way
Sales Conference

10/29/2015

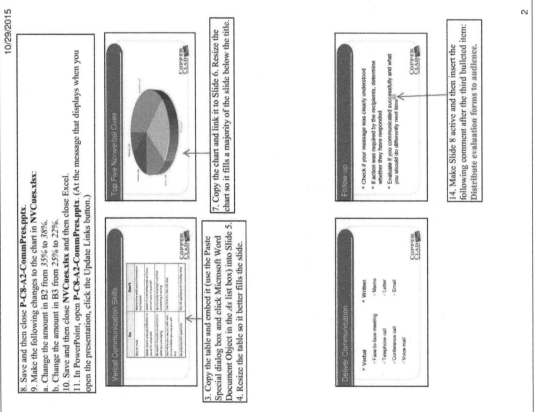

8. Save and then close **P-C8-A2-CommPres.pptx**.

9. Make the following changes to the chart in **NVCues.xlsx**:
   a. Change the amount in B2 from 35% to 38%.
   b. Change the amount in B3 from 25% to 22%.

10. Save and then close **NVCues.xlsx** and then close Excel.

11. In PowerPoint, open **P-C8-A2-CommPres.pptx**. (At the message that displays when you open the presentation, click the Update Links button.)

7. Copy the chart and link it to Slide 6. Resize the chart so it fills a majority of the slide below the title.

3. Copy the table and embed it (use the Paste Special dialog box and click Microsoft Word Document Object in the *As* list box) into Slide 5.

4. Resize the table so it better fills the slide.

14. Make Slide 8 active and then insert the following comment after the third bulleted item: Distribute evaluation forms to audience.

New Products

- Coming in the Spring of 2016:
  - Complete line of homeopathic remedies to combat seasonal allergies
  - Biodegradable cleaning products
  - Website with links to the latest health information resources on the Internet
- Coming in the Fall of 2016:
  - Online shopping
  - Special vitamin and remedy packages

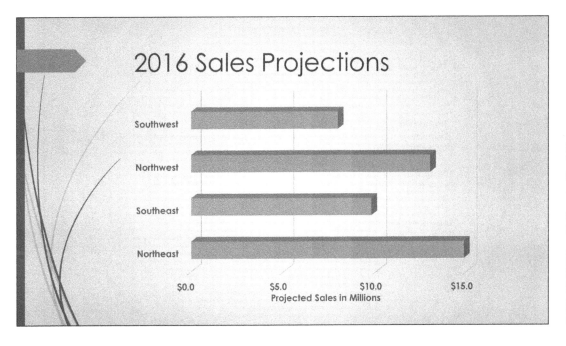

2016 Sales Projections

Southwest

Northwest

Southeast

Northeast

$0.0 $5.0 $10.0 $15.0

Projected Sales in Millions

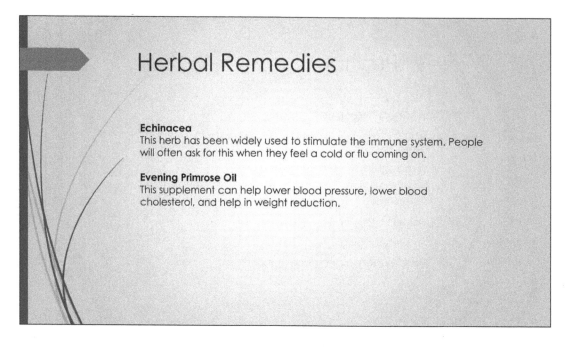

Herbal Remedies

Echinacea
This herb has been widely used to stimulate the immune system. People will often ask for this when they feel a cold or flu coming on.

Evening Primrose Oil
This supplement can help lower blood pressure, lower blood cholesterol, and help in weight reduction.

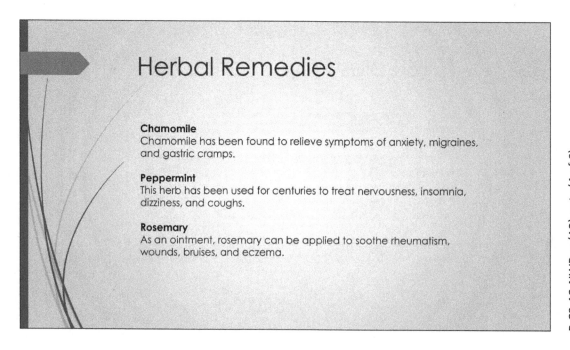

Herbal Remedies

Chamomile
Chamomile has been found to relieve symptoms of anxiety, migraines, and gastric cramps.

Peppermint
This herb has been used for centuries to treat nervousness, insomnia, dizziness, and coughs.

Rosemary
As an ointment, rosemary can be applied to soothe rheumatism, wounds, bruises, and eczema.

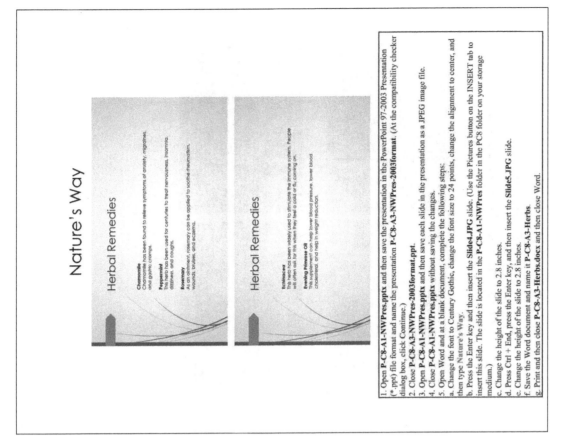

1. Open **P-C8-A1-NWPres.pptx** and then save the presentation in the PowerPoint 97-2003 Presentation (*.ppt) file format and name the presentation **P-C8-A3-NWPres-2003format**. (At the compatibility checker dialog box, click Continue.)
2. Close **P-C8-A3-NWPres-2003format.ppt**.
3. Open **P-C8-A1-NWPres.pptx** and then save each slide in the presentation as a JPEG image file.
4. Close **P-C8-A1-NWPres.pptx** without saving the changes.
5. Open Word and at a blank document, complete the following steps:
a. Change the font to Century Gothic, change the font size to 24 points, change the alignment to center, and then type Nature's Way.
b. Press the Enter key and then insert the **Slide4.JPG** slide. (Use the Pictures button on the INSERT tab to insert this slide. The slide is located in the **P-C8-A1-NWPres** folder in the PC8 folder on your storage medium.)
c. Change the height of the slide to 2.8 inches.
d. Press Ctrl + End, press the Enter key, and then insert the **Slide5.JPG** slide.
e. Change the height of the slide to 2.8 inches.
f. Save the Word document and name it **P-C8-A3-Herbs**.
g. Print and then close **P-C8-A3-Herbs.docx** and then close Word.

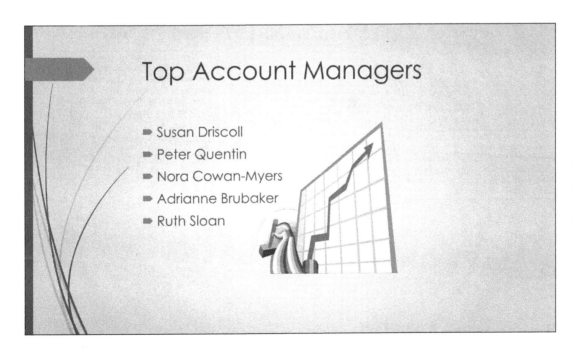

First Choice Travel

Proposed Tour Package Covers

Seattle Tour

Victoria Tour

San Francisco Tour

Portland Tour

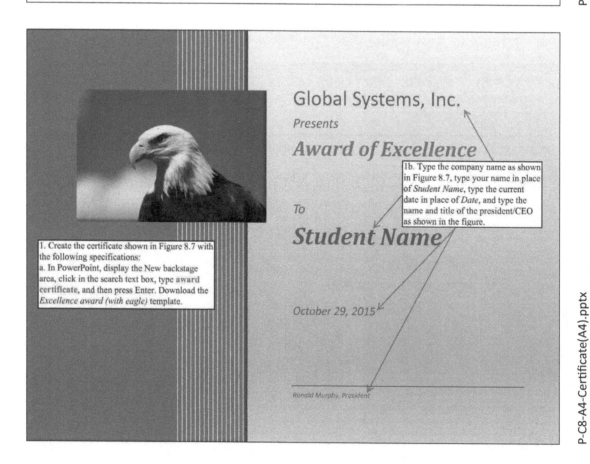

Global Systems, Inc.

Presents

Award of Excellence

To

Student Name

October 29, 2015

Ronald Murphy, President

1. Create the certificate shown in Figure 8.7 with the following specifications:
a. In PowerPoint, display the New backstage area, click in the search text box, type award certificate, and then press Enter. Download the *Excellence award (with eagle)* template.

1b. Type the company name as shown in Figure 8.7, type your name in place of *Student Name*, type the current date in place of *Date*, and type the name and title of the president/CEO as shown in the figure.

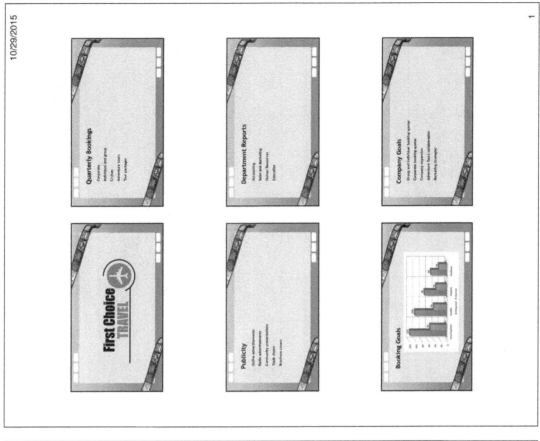

P-C8-VB2-FCTQtrlyMtgPres(VB2,Step8).pptx

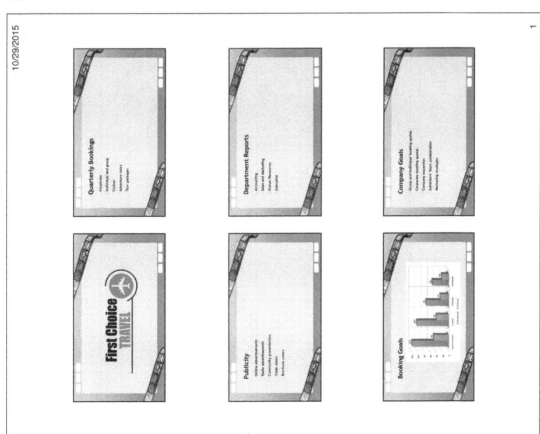

P-C8-VB2-FCTQtrlyMtgPres(VB2,Step3).pptx

Benchmark PowerPoint 2013 Model Answers

Mumps Symptoms
- Fever
- Painful swelling of the salivary glands
- Headache
- Muscle ache
- Tiredness
- Loss of appetite

Transmission of Mumps
- Airborne droplets of saliva and mucus infected with the mumps virus (coughing and sneezing)
- Touching an infected surface and then touching the eyes, nose, or mouth

Mumps
- What are Mumps?
  - Mumps, or epidemic parotitis, is a contagious viral disease

Complications of Mumps
- Most healthy children recover with minimal complications
- Severe complications include:
  - Inflammation of the brain and other organs
  - Sterility in men
  - Mild form of meningitis
  - Spontaneous abortion
  - Deafness

Prevention of Mumps
- Mumps vaccine (contained in the MMR [measles, mumps, and rubella] vaccine)

Chicken Pox
- What is Chicken Pox?
  - A childhood disease caused by the varicella-zoster virus that causes an itchy rash

Complications of Chicken Pox
- Most healthy children recover with no complications
- Complications for high-risk groups of people include:
  - Viral pneumonia
  - Secondary bacterial infections
  - Encephalitis

Prevention of Chicken Pox
- Varicella vaccine

Knowing Childhood Diseases

Symptoms of Chicken Pox
- Initial cold-like symptoms
- High temperature
- Intense itchy rash
- Lesions that generally appear on face, scalp and trunk

Transmission of Chicken pox
- Direct person-to-person contact
- Airborne droplet infection (coughing and sneezing)
- Contact with infected articles such as clothing and bedding

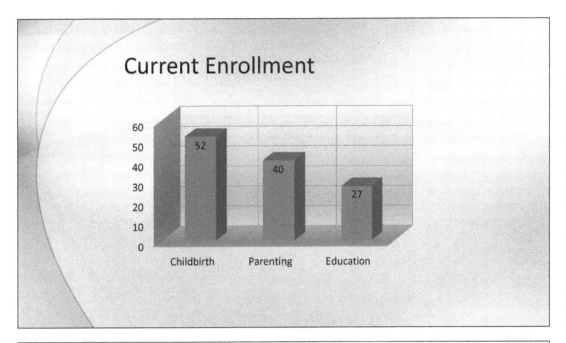

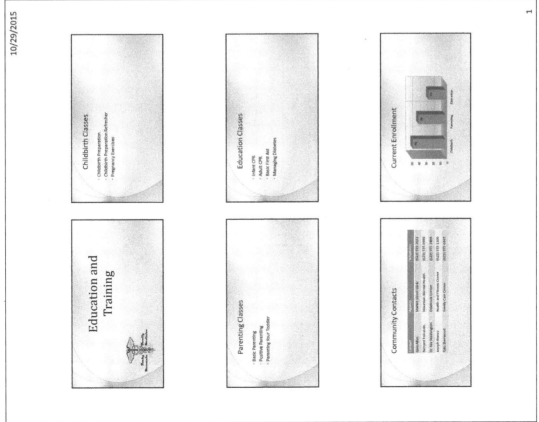

Measles Symptoms

- Cold-like symptoms
- High fever
- Hacking cough
- Fatigue
- Diarrhea
- Sore, red eyes
- Red spots in mouth
- Full body rash

Transmission of Measles

- Spread through the air by a cough or sneeze, and also through sharing food and drink.
- Contagious up to 4 days before and 4 days after the measles rash starts and disappear.

Measles

- What are Measles?
  - A very contagious and easily spread infection also known as rubeola or red measles.

Complications of Measles

- Most healthy children recover with minimal complications
- Severe complications include:
  - Lung infections (pneumonia)
  - Brain swelling (encephalitis)
  - Seizures
  - Miscarriage

Prevention of Measles

- Measles vaccine (contained in the MMR (measles, mumps, and rubella) vaccine)

PowerPoint Performance Assessment 2 Model Answers

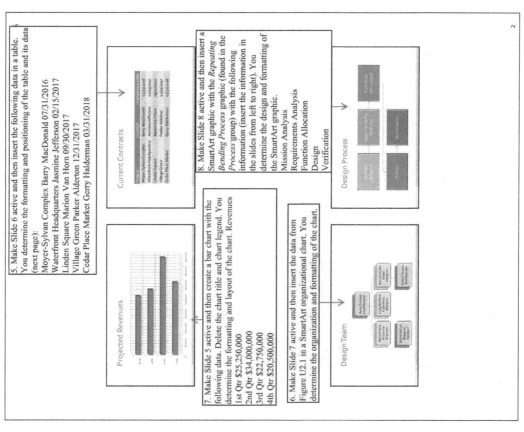

P-U2-A1-GreenDesignPres(A1).pptx (2 of 2)

P-U2-A1-GreenDesignPres(A1).pptx (1 of 2)

10/30/2015

6. Create a footer that prints your first and last names at the bottom of each slide, create a footer for handouts that prints the presentation title *2016 Adventure Packages*, and insert the date in the upper right corner.

1. Open **NortonTravelPres.pptx** and then save the presentation with the name **P-U2-A2-NortonTravelPres**.

4. Display the presentation in Slide Master view and then make the following changes:
a. Click the top slide master thumbnail.
b. Insert an action button in the lower right corner of the slide with the same specifications as those in Step 3.
c. Close Slide Master view.

5. Run the presentation. (Use the action buttons to advance slides. At the last slide, press the Esc key.)

7. Print the presentation as a handout with six slides printed horizontally per page.

2016 Adventure Packages

P-U2-A2-NortonTravelPres(A2).pptx (2 of 2)

10/30/2015

3. Make Slide 1 active and then insert an action button with the following specifications: a. Use the *Action Button: Forward or Next* option to draw the button. b. Draw the button in the lower right corner of the slide and make it approximately one-half inch in size. c. Apply the Subtle Effect - Aqua, Accent 2 shape style.

2. Make Slide 4 active and then create a new Slide 5 (with the Title Only layout) with the following specifications: a. Insert the title *Extreme Adventures* in the slide. b. Open Word and then open **NTExtremeAdventures.docx**. c. Display the Clipboard task pane. (Make sure the task pane is empty. If not, click the Clear All button.) d. Select and then copy *Small Groups*, the paragraph below it, and the blank line below the paragraph. e. Select and then copy *Comprehensive Itineraries*, the paragraph below it, and the blank line below the paragraph. f. Select and then copy *Custom Groups*, the paragraph below it, and the blank line below the paragraph.

2g. Select and then copy *Accommodations*, the paragraph below it, and the blank line below the paragraph. h. Display the **P-U2-A2-NortonTravelPres.pptx** presentation. i. Draw a text box below the title that is approximately 10 inches wide. j. Turn on the display of the Clipboard task pane. k. Paste the *Comprehensive Itineraries* item in the text box in the slide. l. Paste the *Small Groups* item in the text box. m. Paste the *Accommodations* item in the text box. n. Clear and then close the Clipboard. o. Make the **NTExtremeAdventures.docx** document active, close the Clipboard task pane, close the document, and then close Word.

P-U2-A2-NortonTravelPres(A2).pptx (1 of 2)

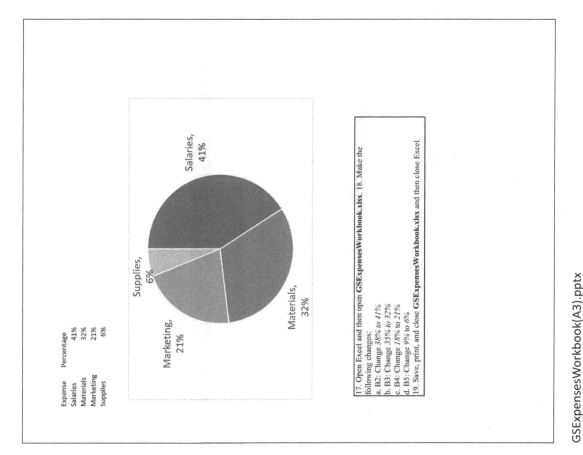

Expense	Percentage
Salaries	41%
Materials	32%
Marketing	21%
Supplies	6%

17. Open Excel and then open **GSExpensesWorkbook.xlsx**. 18. Make the following changes:
a. B2: Change *38% to 41%*
b. B3: Change *35% to 32%*
c. B4: Change *18% to 21%*
d. B5: Change *9% to 6%*
19. Save, print, and close **GSExpensesWorkbook.xlsx** and then close Excel.

GSExpensesWorkbook(A3).pptx

---

1. Open **GSTemplate.pptx**. 3. Save the presentation as a template (to the Custom Office Templates folder) and name the presentation **XXXGSTemplate** (use your initials in place of the *XXX*). 4. Close **XXXGSTemplate.pptx**.
5. Open **XXXGSTemplate.potx**. (To do this, display the New backstage area, click the CUSTOM option, and then double-click the *XXXGSTemplate.potx* thumbnail.) 6. Save the presentation and name it **P-U2-A3-GSMtg**.

2. Display the presentation in Slide Master view, insert **GSLogo.jpg** in the top slide master thumbnail (use the Picture button on the Insert tab to insert the logo), change the height of the logo to one inch, and drag the logo to the lower right corner of the slide master, and then close Slide Master view.

Global Systems

7. Format the first slide with the following specifications: a. Change to the Blank layout. b. Use WordArt to create the text *Global Systems*. (You determine the shape and formatting of the WordArt text.)

10/30/2015

8. Create the second slide with the following specifications: a. Choose the Title Slide layout. b. Type 2016 Sales Meeting as the title. c. Type European Division as the subtitle.

2016 Sales Meeting
European Division

10. Create the fourth slide with the following specifications: a. Choose the Title and Content layout. b. Type Company Goals as the title. c. Type the following as the bulleted items: • Increase product sales by 15 percent • Open a branch office in Spain • Hire one manager and two additional account managers • Decrease production costs by 6 percent

Company Goals
- Increase product sales by 15 percent
- Open a branch office in Spain
- Hire one manager and two additional account managers
- Decrease production costs by 6 percent

12. Create the sixth slide with the following specifications: a. Choose the Title Only layout. b. Type Production Expenses as the title. c. Make Excel the active program and then close **GSWorkbook01.xlsx**. d. Open **GSWorkbook02.xlsx**. e. Save the workbook with Save As and name it **GSExpensesWorkbook**. f. Copy and then link the pie chart in **GSExpensesWorkbook.xlsx** to Slide 6. Size and center the pie chart on the slide. g. Make Excel active, close **GSExpensesWorkbook.xlsx**, and then close Excel.

Production Expenses

13. Run the presentation.
14. Create a footer for handouts that prints the presentation title *2016 Sales Meeting* and insert the date in the upper right corner.
15. Print the presentation as a handout with six slides printed horizontally per page.

Regional Sales

Region	Quota	Actual Sales	Difference
North	$2,350,500	$2,678,450	$327,950
South	$1,900,000	$1,753,405	($146,595)
East	$1,350,900	$1,452,540	$102,040
West	$2,150,000	$2,315,600	$165,600

9. Create the third slide with the following specifications: a. Choose the Title Only layout. b. Type Regional Sales as the title. c. Open Excel and then open **GSWorkbook01.xlsx**. d. Select cells A1 through D5 (the cells containing data) and then copy and embed the cells in Slide 3 as a Microsoft Excel Worksheet Object. e. Increase the size of the cells so they better fill the slide.

Hiring Timeline

Task	Date
Advertising positions	03/01/2016 to 04/30/2016
Review resumes	05/15/2016 to 06/01/2016
Conduct interviews	06/15/2016 to 07/15/2016
Hire personnel	08/01/2016

11. Create the fifth slide with the following specifications: a. Choose the Title and Content layout. b. Type Hiring Timeline as the title. c. Create a table with two columns and five rows and then type the following text in the cells in the table. (You determine the formatting of the cells.) Task Date Advertise positions 03/01/2016 to 04/30/2016 Review resumes 05/15/2016 to 06/01/2016 Conduct interviews 06/15/2016 to 07/15/2016 Hire personnel 08/01/2016

1

P-U2-A3-GSMtg(A3,Step15).pptx

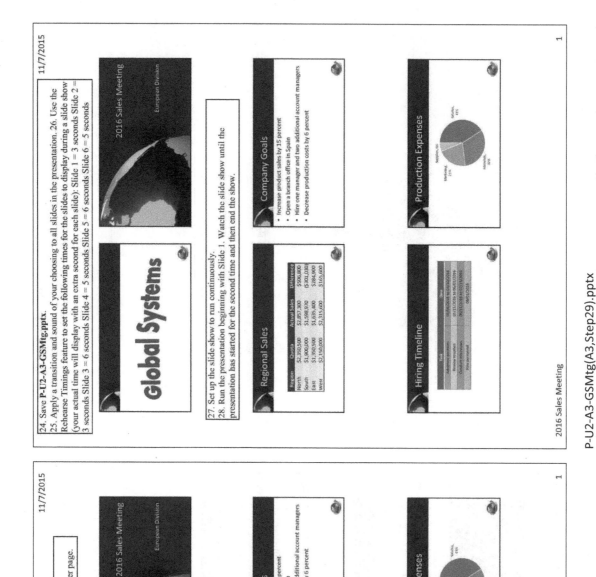

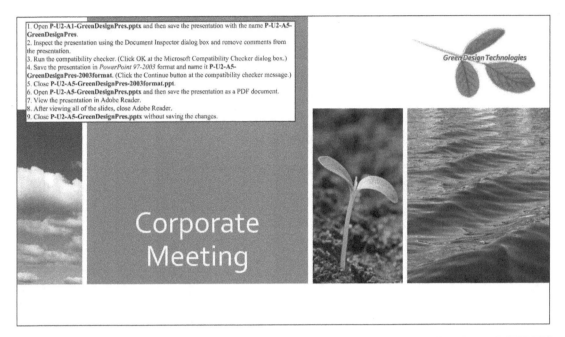

1. Open **P-U2-A1-GreenDesignPres.pptx** and then save the presentation with the name **P-U2-A5-GreenDesignPres**.
2. Inspect the presentation using the Document Inspector dialog box and remove comments from the presentation.
3. Run the compatibility checker. (Click OK at the Microsoft Compatibility Checker dialog box.)
4. Save the presentation in *PowerPoint 97-2003* format and name it **P-U2-A5-GreenDesignPres-2003format**. (Click the Continue button at the compatibility checker message.)
5. Close **P-U2-A5-GreenDesignPres-2003format.ppt**.
6. Open **P-U2-A5-GreenDesignPres.pptx** and then save the presentation as a PDF document.
7. View the presentation in Adobe Reader.
8. After viewing all of the slides, close Adobe Reader.
9. Close **P-U2-A5-GreenDesignPres.pptx** without saving the changes.

Green Design Technologies

Corporate Meeting

P-U2-A4-NTAustralia(A4).pptx

1. Open **NTAustralia.pptx** and then save the presentation with the name **P-U2-A4-NTAustralia**.
3. Display the presentation in Slide Master view and then make the following changes: a. Click the third slide master thumbnail. b. Apply a Fly In entrance animation effect to the title that has the title fly in from the top. c. Apply a Fly In entrance animation effect to the bulleted text that has the text fly in from the left and then dims to a color of your choosing when the next bullet displays. d. Close Slide Master view.

2. With Slide 1 active, apply a Fly In entrance animation effect to the subtitle *Australia Tour* that has the title fly in from the bottom.

6. Save **P-U2-A4-NTAustralia.pptx**.
7. Make Slide 1 active, run the presentation, and then make sure the animation effects play correctly. 8. Print the presentation as a handout with all slides printed horizontally on one page.

4. Make Slide 5 active, select the sun shape that displays above *Sydney*, and then draw a freeform motion path from Sydney to Melbourne, Tasmania, Adelaide, Perth, Derby, Darwin, Cairns, and then back to Sydney. Change the duration to *04.00*.

5. Make Slide 6 active and then make the following changes: a. Click the bottom shape to select it. (You may want to move the top two shapes out of the way.) b. Apply the Grow & Turn entrance effect. c. Click the Add Animation button and then click the *Shrink & Turn* exit effect. d. Click the middle shape to select it and then apply the Grow & Turn entrance effect. e. Click the Add Animation button and then click the *Shrink & Turn* exit effect. f. Click the top shape to select it and then apply the Grow & Turn entrance effect. g. Position the shapes so they are stacked on top of each other so you do not see a portion of the shapes behind.

Past Successes

- Lakeland Hills Subdivision

- Nature's Way Corporate Headquarters

- Redwood Community College, Early Childhood Education Addition

Vision Statement

To design state-of-the-art "smart" buildings with computer-controlled lighting, temperature, air quality, and security systems

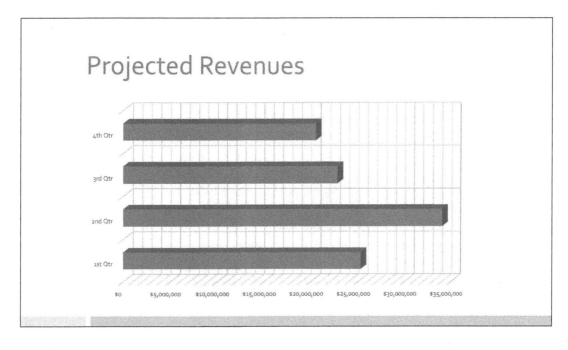

Future Goals

- Increase contract values by $150-170 million
- Open three new satellite offices
  - London, England
  - Toronto, Canada
  - Melbourne, Australia

Design Team

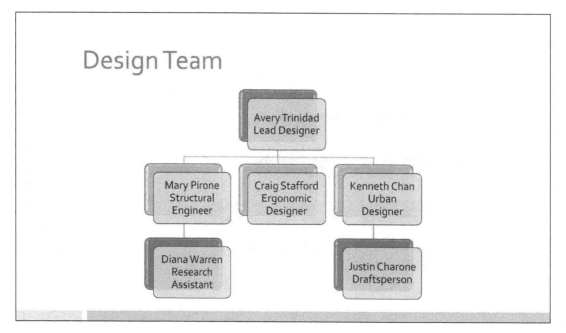

Current Contracts

Project	Contact	Completion Date
Moyer-Sylvan Complex	Barry MacDonald	01/31/2016
Waterfront Headquarters	Jasmine Jefferson	02/15/2017
Linden Square	Marion Van Horn	09/30/2017
Village Green	Parker Alderton	12/31/2017
Cedar Place Market	Gerry Halderman	03/31/2018

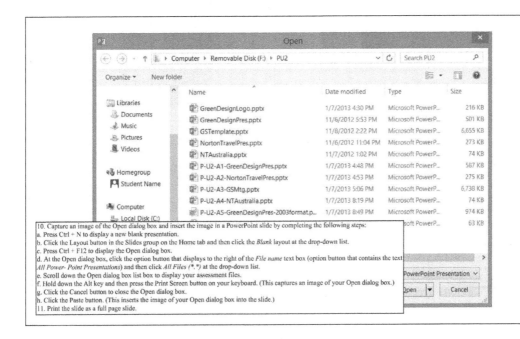

10. Capture an image of the Open dialog box and insert the image in a PowerPoint slide by completing the following steps:
a. Press Ctrl + N to display a new blank presentation.
b. Click the Layout button in the Slides group on the Home tab and then click the *Blank* layout at the drop-down list.
c. Press Ctrl + F12 to display the Open dialog box.
d. At the Open dialog box, click the option button that displays to the right of the *File name* text box (option button that contains the text *All Power- Point Presentations*) and then click *All Files (*.*)* at the drop-down list.
e. Scroll down the Open dialog box list box to display your assessment files.
f. Hold down the Alt key and then press the Print Screen button on your keyboard. (This captures an image of your Open dialog box.)
g. Click the Cancel button to close the Open dialog box.
h. Click the Paste button. (This inserts the image of your Open dialog box into the slide.)
11. Print the slide as a full page slide.

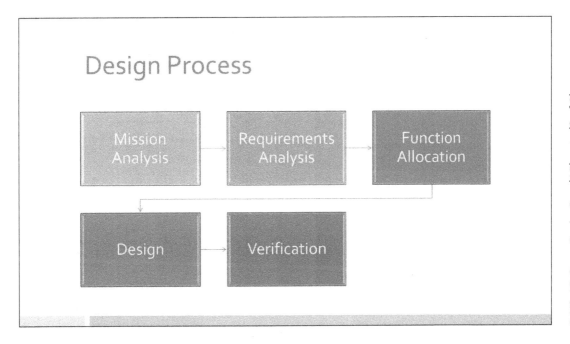

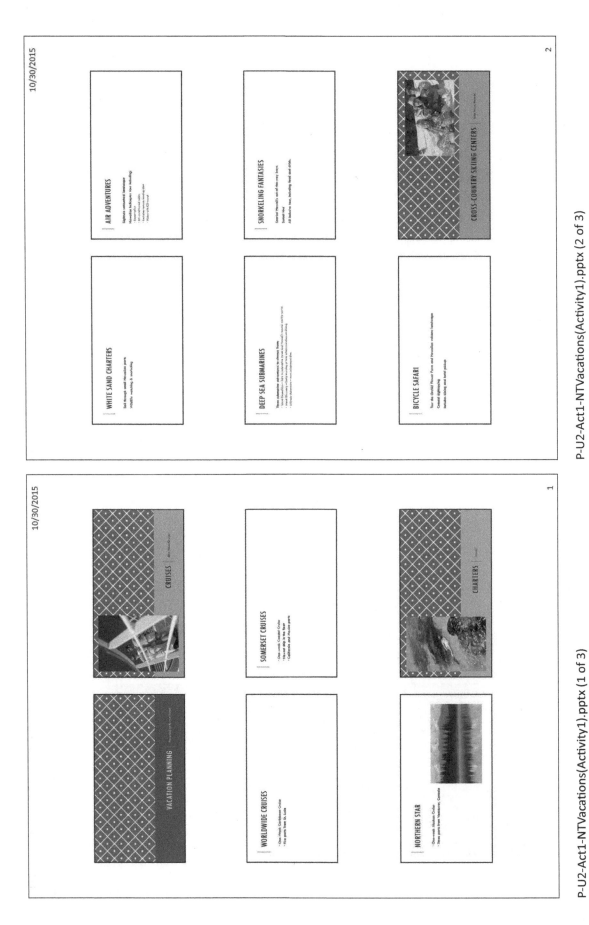

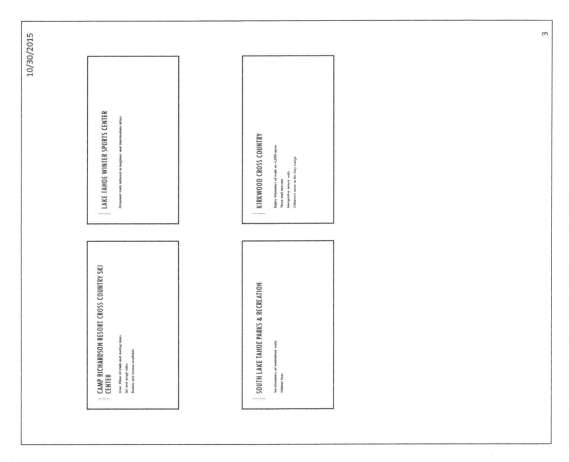

P-U2-Act1-NTVacations(Activity1).pptx (3 of 3)

Rubrics

Benchmark PowerPoint 2013 Level 1, Chapter 1

Note that the following are suggested rubrics. Instructors should feel free to customize the rubric to suit their grading standards and/or to adjust the point values.

Suggested Scoring Distribution: Above average = student completes 80% or more of task(s); average = student completes 70–79% of task(s); below average = student completes 69% or less of task(s)

PowerPoint, Chapter 1

Skills Check

Assessment 1: Create a Presentation on Types of Resumes
File: **P-C1-A1-ResumeTypes.pptx**

Steps	Tasks	Criteria	Value	Score
1a-1b	Selecting Theme	Open PowerPoint; create presentation with the text shown in Figure 1.10; Select *FILE* then the *New* option. At the backstage area, click the *Word Type* theme; click the variant in the top row in the second column, then click the *Create* button.	2	
1c	Creating Slides	Create slides and type text shown in Fig. 1.10. Select *Title Slide* layout for slides 1 and 5; then use the **Title** and **Content** layout for slides 2, 3, and 4.	6	
2	Saving	Save the completed presentation in PC1 folder on your storage medium and name the presentation as **P-C1-A1-ResumeTypes. pptx**	4	
3-6	Applying Transitions and Sound	Apply the *Push* transition (located in the *Subtle* section) with a From Left effect to all slides in the presentation. Change transition speed to 01.50 seconds. Apply the *Wind* sound to all slides in the presentation. Run the presentation.	6	
7-8	Printing and Saving	Print as handout with six slides horizontally per page Save presentation as **P-C1-A1-ResumeTypes.pptx**	2	
		TOTAL POINTS	20	

Assessment 2: Create a Presentation on Preparing a Company Newsletter Presentation
File: **P-C1-A2-Newsletter.pptx**

Steps	Tasks	Criteria	Value	Score
1-3	Creating Slides	At a blank screen, click the *FILE* tab and then click the *New* option. At the *New* backstage area, click the *Blank Presentation* template. Create slides and type text shown in Fig. 1.11 on page 40.	6	
4-5	Selecting Theme	Apply the **Basis** design theme and the **Orange** variant (third thumbnail in the Variants group). Run presentation.	2	
6	Printing	Print as handout with six slides horizontally per page.	4	
7-8	Formatting	Apply the **Parallax** design theme and the **Red** variant (fourth thumbnail in the Variants group). Add the **Switch** transition (located in the *Exciting* section) with a **Left** effect to all slides. Add the **Camera** sound to all slides Advance all slides automatically after five seconds. Run presentation.	6	
9-10	Saving, Closing	Save presentation as **P-C1-A2-Newsletter**. Close **P-C1-A2-Newsletter.pptx** presentation.	2	
		TOTAL POINTS	20	

Visual Benchmark

Create a Presentation on Preparing a Newsletter
File: **P-C1-VB-Interview.pptx**

Steps	Tasks	Criteria	Value	Score
1a	Selecting Theme	Create presentation shown in Figure 1.12 with the **Organic** design theme template and apply appropriate variant.	2	
1b	Creating Slides	Create slides and type text shown in Fig. 1.12 (reading from left to right).	8	
1c	Formatting	Apply transition, sound, and transition duration of student's choosing to each slide in the presentation.	6	
2-3	Saving, Running	Save the presentation as **P-C1-VB-Interview**. Run presentation.	2	
4-5	Printing, Closing	Print as handout with six slides horizontally per page. Close **P-C1-VB-Interview.pptx** presentation.	2	
		TOTAL POINTS	20	

Case Study

Part 1

File: **P-C1-CS-P1-PPSmokeDetectors.pptx**

Steps	Tasks	Criteria	Value	Score
1	Opening Word File	Open **PPSmokeDetectors.docx**. Read document.	2	
2	Creating Slides	Use the information in the *Planning a Presentation* section and create at least five slides.	10	
3	Formatting	Apply an appropriate design theme. Add transition to all slides. Add sound to all slides.	11	
4	Saving, Printing	Save presentation as **P-C1-CS-P1-PPSmokeDetectors**. Print as handout with all slides on one page.	2	
		TOTAL POINTS	25	

Part 2

File: **P-C1-CS-P1-PPSmokeDetectors.pptx**

Steps	Tasks	Criteria	Value	Score
1	Printing	Use Help to learn about printing in grayscale. Print the **P-C1-CS-P1-PPSmokeDetectors** presentation in grayscale with two slides per page.	5	
		TOTAL POINTS	5	

Part 3

File: **P-C1-CS-P1-PPSmokeDetectors.pptx**

Steps	Tasks	Criteria	Value	Score
1	Research, Inserting Slide	Use the Internet for online stores that sell smoke detectors. Open **P-C1-CS-P1-PPSmokeDetectors**. Insert new slide with the following information: • Names of stores • Web addresses • Other important information	6	
2	Saving, Printing	Save presentation. Print in **Outline** view. Close **P-C1-CS-P1-PPSmokeDetectors.pptx** presentation.	4	
		TOTAL POINTS	10	

Benchmark PowerPoint 2013 Level 1, Chapter 2

Skills Check

Assessment 1: Create an Electronic Design Presentation

File: **P-C2-A1-ElecDesign.pptx**

Steps	Tasks	Criteria	Value	Score
1	Selecting Theme, Creating Slides	Create presentation shown in Figure 2.6 using the **Wisp** design theme and the second variant. (When typing bulleted text, press the Tab key to move the insertion point to the desired tab level).	7	
2-4	Spell Check, Saving	Complete spell check on all slides Save presentation into PC2 folder on storage medium, name as **P-C2-A1-ElecDesign.pptx**. Run the presentation.	2	
5	Printing	Print as handout with four slides horizontally per page.	1	
6-7	Editing, Saving	Change presentation: a. Using Slider Sorter view, move Slide 3 between Slides 1 and 2. b. Move Slide 4 between Slides 2 and 3. c. Change to Normal view. d. Search for the word *document* and replace with *brochure*. (After the replacements, make Slide 1 active and, if necessary capitalize the 'b' in 'brochure' on Slide 1. e. Add the *Uncover* transition and *Hammer* sound to each slide. f. Save presentation.	5	
8-11	Reuse Slides	Using the **Reuse Slides** task pane, browse to the PC2 folder on your storage medium, double-click *LayoutTips.pptx* . Insert the *Layout Punctuation Tips* slide below Slide 4. Insert the *Layout Tips* slide below Slide 5. Close the **Reuse** Slides task pane.	4	
12	Replacing Text	Find all occurrences of *Layout* and replace with *Design*. Use *Match case*.	2	
13-14	Moving Slides	Move Slide 5 between Slides 1 and 2. Move Slide 6 between Slides 2 and 3.	2	
15	Saving	Change to Normal view and save presentation.	1	
16	Printing	Print handout with six slides horizontally per page.	2	
17-18	Creating Sections	Beginning with slide 2, create section named *Design Tips*. Beginning with slide 4, create section named *Design Features*.	2	
19-20	Printing Section, Saving	Print only *Design Features* section as handout with four slides horizontally per page. Save and close **P-C2-A1-ElecDesign.pptx**.	2	
		TOTAL POINTS	30	

Assessment 2: Create a Netiquette Presentation
File: **P-C2-A2-InternetApps.pptx**

Steps	Tasks	Criteria	Value	Score
1-2	Creating Slides, Applying Theme	Create slides, select slide layout, and type text shown in Fig. 2-7. Apply the **Organic** design theme and the fourth variant (in the variants group). Size and move placeholders for attractive positioning, if necessary.	6	
3	Duplicating Slides	Select Slides 4 through 6; duplicate slides.	2	
4	Inserting Text	In slide 7, select the placeholder netiquette rule text and type: **Do not plagiarize.** In slide 8, select the netiquette rule text in placeholder and type: **Respect and accept people's differences.** In Slide 9, select the netiquette rule text in the placeholder and type: **Respect others' time**.	4	
5	Spell Check	Complete spell check on text in the presentation.	2	
6-7	Saving, Printing	Save presentation as **P-C2-A2-InternetApps**. Print as handout with six slides horizontally per page.	1	
8	Editing	Display presentation in Slide Sorter view. Move Slide 3 between Slide 5 and Slide 6. Move Slide 7 between Slide 3 and Slide 4.	2	
9	Formatting	Add the Split transition, the Click sound and change the duration to 01.00 second for all slides in the presentation.	2	
10-13	Saving, Printing, Closing	Save presentation. Run presentation. Print presentation handout with nine slides horizontally per page. Close **P-C2-A2-InternetApps.pptx** presentation.	1	
		TOTAL POINTS	20	

Assessment 3: Download a Design Theme
File: **P-C2-A3-InternetApps.pptx**

Steps	Tasks	Criteria	Value	Score
1-2	Downloading Design Theme	Connect to the Internet. Display New tab in Backstage view and search the *Office.com Templates* heading for Digital blue tunnel presentation, (widescreen), select, then click the Create button.	1	
3	Opening File	After downloading design theme, apply design theme. Open **P-C2-A2-InternetApps.pptx**.	2	
4-6	Copying, Pasting	Select the nine slides in the **PC2A2InternetApps.pptx** presentation and click on Copy. Click on PowerPoint button on the Taskbar. Click on the thumbnail representing downloaded design theme applied. Paste the nine slides in the current presentation.	2	
7	Deleting	Delete Slide 1, and then select and delete Slides 10 through 19.	1	
8	Formatting	Scroll through presentation. Make changes to position text attractively on each slide.	2	

Steps	Tasks	Criteria	Value	Score
9-12	Saving, Printing, Closing	Save presentation as **P-C2-A3-InternetApps**. Run presentation. Print as handout with nine slides horizontally per page. Close both presentations **PC2A3-InternetApps.pptx** and **PC2A2InternetApps.pptx**.	2	
		TOTAL POINTS	10	

Visual Benchmark

Formatting a Presentation on Online Learning

File: **P-C2-VB-OnlineLearning.pptx**

Steps	Tasks	Criteria	Value	Score
1	Opening, Saving	Open **OnlineLearning.pptx** in the PC2 folder. Save as **P-C2-VB-OnlineLearning**.	1	
2	Formatting	Format presentation as illustrated in Fig. 2.8 with the following specifications: a. Apply the **Parallex** design theme and the fourth variant. b. Use the *Reuse Slides* option to insert the last two additional slides from the **Learning.pptx** presentation. c. Arrange slides to match illustration in Fig. 2.8 with slides reading from left to right. d. Size and/or move placeholders to match slides in Fig. 2.8	4	
3-4	Formatting	Apply transition and sound of student's choosing to each slide. Run presentation.	4	
5-6	Printing, Saving	Print as handout with six slides horizontally per page. Save and close **P-C2-VB-OnlineLearning.pptx**.	1	
		TOTAL POINTS	10	

Case Study

Part 1

File: **P-C2-CS-JobAnalysis.pptx**

Steps	Tasks	Criteria	Value	Score
1	Opening, Saving	Open **JobAnalysis.pptx**. Save as **P-C2-CS-JobAnalysis.pptx**	1	
2	Formatting	• Make modifications to maintain consistency in size and location of placeholders using Reset button. • Maintain consistency in heading text. • Move text from overcrowded slide to new slide. • Complete spelling check. • Apply design theme. • Make other modifications to improve presentation.	8	
5	Saving	Save **P-C2-CS-JobAnalysis.pptx**.	1	

Steps	Tasks	Criteria	Value	Score
		TOTAL POINTS	**10**	

Part 2

File: **P-C2-CS-ResumePres.pptx**

Steps	Tasks	Criteria	Value	Score
1	Opening, Copying	Open the **ResumePres.pptx** presentation. Copy Slides 2 and 3 into **P-C2-CS-JobAnalysis.pptx** presentation at end of presentation.	2	
2	Researching and Creating Slides	Locate information on the Internet with tips on writing a resume. Create one or two slides with the information. Format slides appropriately.	5	
3	Formatting	Add transition and sound to all slides in presentation.	2	
4	Saving	Save the **P-C2-CS-JobAnalysis.pptx** presentation.	1	
		TOTAL POINTS	**10**	

Part 3

File: **P-C2-CS-JobAnalysis.pptx**

Steps	Tasks	Criteria	Value	Score
1	Using Word, Researching	Open Word, blank document template. Select *File*, *New*. In Backstage view, display *Office.com Templates* and search *resume*; experiment with downloading a template.	3	
2	Creating and Proofreading Slide	With **P-C2-CS-JobAnalysis.pptx** open, add additional slide at end of presentation providing steps on how to download a resume in Microsoft Word.	5	
3	Saving, Printing	Print as handout with six slides horizontally to a page. Save, run, and close **P-C2-CS-JobAnalysis.pptx** presentation.	2	
		TOTAL POINTS	**10**	

Benchmark PowerPoint 2013 Level 1, Chapter 3

Skills Check

Assessment 1: Create, Format, and Modify a Benefits Presentation

File: **P-C3-A1-Benefits.pptx**

Steps	Tasks	Criteria	Value	Score
1	Create Slides	Create slides and type text shown in Fig. 3.12.	5	
2	Applying Theme	Apply the *Facet* design theme and then apply the *blue variant*.	1	

Steps	Tasks	Criteria	Value	Score
3	Editing, Formatting	Format Slide 1: • Select title *BENEFITS PROGRAM* and change font to *Candara, font size to 60 points*, apply the *Turquoise, Accent 1, Darker 50% font color*, apply italic formatting • Select subtitle *Changes to Plans* and change font to *Candara*, font size to 32 points, apply the *Turquoise, Accent 1 font* color, and apply bold and shadow formatting • Click the title placeholder and then click the **Center** button in the paragraph group. Center the subtitle in the placeholder.	4	
4	Editing, Formatting	Format Slide 2: • Select title *INTRODUCTION* and change font to *Candara*, font size to 44, apply shadow formatting • Using Format Painter, apply the *Turquoise, Accent 1, Darker 50%* font color, and apply shadow formatting. Use the Format Painter and apply the title formatting to the titles in the remaining slides.	3	
5	Centering	Center-align and middle-align the titles in Slides 2 through 5.	2	
6-9	Line Spacing	Change line spacing on the following slides: • Slide 2, select bulleted text and change to 2.0. • Slide 3, select bulleted text and change to 2.0. • Slide 4, select bulleted text and change to 1.5. • Slide 5, select bulleted text and change spacing after paragraphs to 18 pt. (Use Paragraph dialog box.)	4	
10-13	Formatting Bulleted Items	Change Slide 2 bullets: • Numbering 1, 2, 3 option • Font size to 90% • Apply the *Turquoise, Accent 1, Darker 50%* color, and then close the dialog box Change Slide 3 bullets: • Numbering 1, 2, 3 option • Font size to 90% • Apply the *Turquoise, Accent 1, Darker 50%* color, change the starting number to 5, and then close the dialog box. Change Slide 4 and Slide 5 bullets: • *Hollow Square Bullets*	4	
14-15	Saving, Printing	Save presentation as **P-C3-A1-Benefits**. Print handout with six slides horizontally per page.	2	
16-17	Formatting	Apply the *Organic* design theme. Apply transition and sound of student's choosing to each slide.	4	
18-20	Running, Printing, Saving, Closing	Run presentation. Print handout with six slides horizontally per page. Save and close **P-C3-A1-Benefits.pptx**.	1	
		TOTAL POINTS	30	

Assessment 2: Format and Modify a Perennials Presentation
File: **P-C3-A2-PerennialsPres.pptx**

Steps	Tasks	Criteria	Value	Score
1	Opening, Saving	Open **PerennialsPres.pptx**. Save As **P-C3-A2-PerennialsPres**.	1	
2	Formatting	Format Slide 3: Format the bulleted text into two columns Change line spacing to double spacing (2.0). Each column contains four bulleted items Display the Paragraph dialog box, change the *By* option (in the *Indentation* section) to 0.4. Close the dialog box.	4	
3	Formatting	Format Slide 2: click anywhere in the bulleted text, click the Drawing group task pane launcher and then make the following changes at the *Format Shape* task page: • With the Fill & Line icon selected, click *FILL* to expand the options, click the *Gradient fill* option, change *Type* to Rectangular, and then change *Color* to *Green, Accent 1, Lighter 60%* (fifth column, third row in the Theme Colors section), • Click the Effects icon, click the **SHADOW** option, click the *Presets* button, and then click the *Offset Right* option (first column, second row) • Click the Size & Properties icon and then click *TEXT BOX* to expand the options. • Change the left margin measurement to 1-inch and the top margin to 0.4-inch. • Close the task pane.	4	
4	Formatting	Slide 1: Click the subtitle placeholder, and then apply the following shape and outline fill: • Click the *Shape Fill* button arrow on **HOME** tab and then click the *Eyedropper* option. • Point the eyedropper to the light green border at the top of the slide and then click the left mouse button. • Click the *Shape Outline* button arrow and then click the *Eyedropper* option. • Position the tip of the eyedropper on a yellow colored flower in the *Greenspace Architects* logo and then click the left mouse button.	4	
5	Formatting	Slide 2: Click the DESIGN tab, click the *Format Background* button, and then apply the following formatting: At the Format Background task pane with the *Fill* icon selected, click the *Solid Fill* option. Click the *Color* button and then click the *Aqua, Accent 5 Lighter 80%* option (ninth column, second row in the *Theme Colors* section) Click the *Apply to All* button and close the Task pane	4	
6-7	Printing, Organization	Print the presentation with six slides printed horizontally per page. Add a transition and sound of your choosing to all slides.	2	
8-9	Finishing	Run the presentation, Save and close **P-C3-A2-PerennialsPres.pptx**.	1	
		TOTAL POINTS	20	

Assessment 3: Create and Apply a Custom Theme to a Travel Presentation
File: **P-C3-A3-TravelEngland.pptx**

Steps	Tasks	Criteria	Value	Score
1	Applying Design Theme	At a blank presentation, apply the *Parallax* design theme.	2	
2	Creating Custom Theme Colors	Create custom theme colors named with student's first and last name that change the following colors: • At the *Create New Theme Colors* dialog box, change the *Text/Background Light 2* option to *Red, Accent 4, Lighter 80%.* (eighth column, second row in the *Theme Colors* section). • Change the Accent 1 option to *Red, Accent 4, Darker 50%* (eighth column, bottom row in the *Theme Colors* section).	4	
3	Creating Custom Theme Fonts	Create custom theme fonts named with student's first and last name that apply the following fonts: • Change the *Heading font* to *Copperplate Gothic Bold.* • Change the *Body font* to *Rockwell.*	4	
4	Saving Theme	Save current theme as custom theme named with student's first and last names. (Save Current Theme dialog box).	2	
5	Closing	Close current presentation without saving.	1	
6	Opening, Saving	Open **TravelEngland.pptx**. Save as **P-C3-A3-TravelEngland**.	1	
7	Applying Theme	Apply student's custom theme with your first and last names.	2	
8	Formatting	Improve visual appeal of Slides 2 and 3 by increasing the spacing between items and positioning bulleted item placeholders attractively in slides.	2	
9	Formatting	Format Slide 4 by increasing spacing between items, format text into two columns with each column containing three bulleted items (suggested decreasing size of placeholder).	2	
10	Formatting	Format Slides 5 and 6 into two columns with four bulleted items in each column (suggested decreasing size of placeholder).	4	
11	Printing	Print as handout with six slides horizontally per page.	2	
12	Formatting	Add a transition of choosing to all slides. Add sound of choosing to slides.	2	
13-16	Running, Saving, Closing	Run presentation. Save presentation as **P-C3-A3-TravelEngland.pptx**. Display a blank presentation and then delete the custom theme colors, custom theme fonts, and custom theme created for this assessment. Close presentation without saving it	2	
		TOTAL POINTS	30	

Assessment4: Prepare a Presentation on Online Shopping

File: **P-C3-A4-OnlineShopping.pptx**

Steps	Tasks	Criteria	Value	Score
1-3	Opening, Printing, and Close a Word Document	Open Word and open the **OnlineShopping.docx** document, located in the PC3 folder of your storage medium. Print the document by clicking the *FILE* tab, clicking the *Print* option, and then clicking the Print button at the Print backstage area. Close the document and exit Word.	2	
4	Creating a Presentation	Based on the information provided in the Word document, create a presentation with the following specifications: • Create a title slide and insert student name as subtitle. • Create Slides summarizing Word document. Student determines number of slides. (Be careful not to overcrowd each slide with text) • Proofread and correct errors. • Apply design theme of student's choosing. • Apply transition and sound of student's choosing to all slides.	6	
5-6	Saving, Running Presentation	Save presentation as **P-C3-A4-OnlineShopping.pptx**. Run presentation.	1	
7-8	Printing, Closing	Print as handout with six slides horizontally per page. Close **P-C3-A4-OnlineShopping.pptx** presentation.	1	
		TOTAL POINTS	10	

Visual Benchmark

Format a Presentation on Home Safety

File: **P-C3-VB-HomeSafety.pptx**

Steps	Tasks	Criteria	Value	Score
1	Opening, Saving	Open **HomeSafety.pptx**. Save as **P-C3-VB-HomeSafety**.	1	

Steps	Tasks	Criteria	Value	Score
2	Formatting	Format presentation as illustrated in Fig. 3.13 with the following specifications: a. Apply the *Facet design* theme, and the *blue variant* color. b. Delete and rearrange slides as shown in the figure. c. Apply the *Parchment* texture slide background and change the slide *background transparency to 50%* for all slides in the presentation. (Apply these options using the Format Background task pane). d. Change the font size of the title in Slide 1 to 60 points, apply bold formatting, apply the *Blue, Accent 2, Darker 25%* Font color and center align the title. e. Change the font size of the subtitles in Slide 1 to 28 points, apply italics, change the font color to *Turquoise, Accent 1, Darker 25%* and center align the subtitle. f. Change the font size of the titles in Slides 2 through 6 to 48 points and the font color to *Turquoise, Accent 1, Darker 50%*. g. Change line spacing, spacing after, column formatting and bullet styles so your slides display in a manner similar to slides in Fig. 3.13. h. Select the bulleted text placeholder in Slide 6, display the **Format Shape** task pane, select the *Solid fill* option, and then change the color to *Turquoise, Accent 1, Lighter 80%*. Display the Format Shape task pane with the **TEXT OPTIONS** tab selected and the Textbook icon selected. Change left margin to 1-inch; top margin to 0.2-inch.	8	
3-4	Printing, Saving	Print as handout with six slides horizontally per page. Save and close **P-C3-VB-HomeSafety**.	1	
		TOTAL POINTS	10	

Case Study

Part 1

File: **P-C3-CS-LunchMenu.pptx**

Steps	Tasks	Criteria	Value	Score
1	Opening, Printing, and Closing	Open Word and the **LunchMenu.docx** file. Print document. Close document.	1	
2	Creating, Proofreading Presentation	Based on the information provided in the Word document, create a PowerPoint presentation by displaying the *New* backstage area. Search for the *Fresh food* presentation design theme template on Office.com that contains vegetables on the title slide Proofread and correct errors.	16	
2	Formatting	Improve visual appeal with formatting changes.	2	
5	Saving	Save as **P-C3-CS-LunchMenu**.	1	
		TOTAL POINTS	20	

Part 2

File: **P-C3-CS-LunchMenu.pptx**

Steps	Tasks	Criteria	Value	Score
1	Creating Custom Theme Colors, Saving Custom Theme	With **P-C3-CS-LunchMenu.pptx** open, create custom theme colors: • *Text/Background –Light 1 color to Gold, Accent 2, Lighter 80%* • *Accent 3 color to Blue, Accent 5, Darker 25%.* Create custom theme fonts: • *Monotype Corsiva* as heading font • *Garamond* as body font Save custom theme as *LaDolce Vita* followed by student's initials.	6	
3	Formatting	Add transition and sound to all slides in presentation.	2	
4	Printing and Saving	Print as handout with six slides horizontally per page. Save and close **P-C3-CS-LunchMenu.pptx** presentation.	2	
		TOTAL POINTS	10	

Part 3

File: **P-C3-CS-RestMenus.pptx**

Steps	Tasks	Criteria	Value	Score
1	Researching	Using the Internet, search the following: Two companies that print restaurant menus Two companies that design restaurant menus Names of two restaurant menu design software programs.	2	
2	Creating and Proofreading	Proofread and correct errors.	5	
3	Formatting	Apply design theme downloaded in Part 1. Format slides to improve visual appeal. Add transition and sound to all slides in presentation.	2	
4	Saving, Printing	Save presentation as **P-C3-CS-RestMenu.pptx**. Print as handout with six slides horizontally to a page. Close presentation.	1	
		TOTAL POINTS	10	

Part 4

File: **P-C3-CS-RestMenus.pptx**

Steps	Tasks	Criteria	Value	Score
1	Researching	Using PowerPoint Help feature, learn how to insert a hyperlinking of a slide to a web page or website.	1	
2	Creating Hyperlinks	Create at least two hyperlinks between sites listed in the presentation and the web page or website.	3	

Steps	Tasks	Criteria	Value	Score
3	Printing, Saving	Print slide(s) containing hyperlinks. Save and close **P-C3-CS-RestMenu.pptx** presentation.	1	
		TOTAL POINTS	5	

Benchmark PowerPoint 2013 Level 1, Chapter 4

Skills Check

Assessment 1: Format and Add Enhancements to a Travel Presentation

File: **P-C4-A1-TravelEngland.pptx**

Steps	Tasks	Criteria	Value	Score
1	Opening, Saving	Open **TravelEngland.pptx**. Save As **P-C4-A1-TravelEngland**.	1	
2	Formatting	Slide 8: Insert the slide shown in Figure 4.13 with the following changes: a. Insert a new slide with the *Title* only layout b. Type the title *Travel England* as shown in the slide c. Draw a text box in the slide. Type the text shown in Figure 4.13. Select and then change the text font size to 40 points and apply the *Tan, Background 2, Darker 75%* font color. d. Apply the *Tan, Background 2, Darker 10%* shape fill to the text box. e. Apply the *Dark Teal, 8 pt. glow, Accent color 4 shape effect* (from the Glow side menu). f. Display the Format Shape task pane with the Size & Properties icon selected, change height to 2.8 inches, the width 9 inches (in the SIZE section). Change the left, right, top and bottom margins to 0.4 inch (in the TEXT BOX section). Close the Format Shape task pane. g. Distribute the text box horizontally and vertically on the slide. (Use the Align button on DRAWING TOOLS FORMAT tab)	5	
3	Setting Tabs	Slide 2: Select the text in the text box and then set a left tab at the 0.5-inch mark, a center tab at the 6-inch mark, and a right tab at the 9.5-inch mark. Bold the headings in the first row.	1	
4	Formatting	Slide 6: Select the picture, make the following changes: a. Use the Corrections button on the PICTURE TOOLS FORMAT tab to sharpen the image 25%. b. Display the Format Picture task pane with the Size & Properties icon selected. c. Change the scale height to 150%, the horizontal position to 5.5 inches, the vertical position to 2.2 inches, and then close the task pane.	3	

Steps	Tasks	Criteria	Value	Score
5	Formatting	Slide 4: Make the following changes: Insert the picture Stonehenge.jpg (PC4 folder) a. Crop the picture to display as shown in Fig. 4.14 b. Send the picture behind the text c. Size and move the picture so it displays as shown in Fig. 4.14 d. Size and move the bulleted text placeholder so it displays as shown in figure	2	
6	Inserting and Formatting Picture	Slide 7: Insert clip art image as shown in Figure 4.15 with the following specifications: a. At Insert Pictures window, search for *green umbrella* and then download the umbrella image shown in Fig 4.15. b. Flip the umbrella horizontally (Rotate button) c. Correct image to *Brightness, -40% Contrast +20%* d. Change height of image to 4-inches. e. Change horizontal position to 6.8 inches, vertical position to 2-inches at the Format Picture task pane with the Size & Properties icon selected.	5	
7	Inserting Clip Art Image, Formatting	Slide 8: display the Format Background task pane (Format background button on the DESIGN tab) Insert the picture shown in Figure 4.16 with the following specifications: a. Insert the picture named **BigBen.jpg** (located in the PC4 folder) using the File button on the Format Background task pane with the Fill icon selected). b. Click the Fill icon in the Format Background task pane and then change the *Offset top* option to -30% and the *Offset bottom* option to -125%. c. Display the Format background task pane with the Picture icon selected d. Change the sharpness to 25% and the contrast to 30% e. Size and move the text in placeholders so the text is positioned as shown in Figure 4.16	5	
8	Inserting and Formatting Shapes	Slide 9: Insert a new slide with the Title only layout. Insert the title and insert and format a shape as shown in Figure 4.17 with the following specifications: a. Type the title Travel Discounts! as shown in Figure 4.17 b. Draw the shape shown in the slide using the Horizontal Scroll shape c. Change the height of the shape to 5 inches and the width to 10 inches d. Apply the Subtle Effect - Dark Teal, Accent 4 shape style to the shape e. Type the text in the shape as shown in the figure. Change the font size for the text to 36 points; apply the Tan, Background 2, Darker 75% font color, turn on bold formatting. f. Distribute the shape horizontally and vertically on the slide	5	
9-11	Formatting	Apply the *Peel Off* transition to each slide and insert slide numbers on each slide. Insert a footer for notes and handouts pages that prints your first and last name.	2	

Steps	Tasks	Criteria	Value	Score
12-14	Run, print and saving	Run the presentation, print the presentation as a handout with six slides printed horizontally per page. Save and close **P-C4-A1-TravelEngland.pptx**	1	
		TOTAL POINTS	30	

Assessment 2: Format and Add Enhancements to a Gardening Presentation
File: **P-C4-A2-GreenspacePres.pptx**

Steps	Tasks	Criteria	Value	Score
1	Opening, Saving	Open **GreenspacePres.pptx**. Save As **P-C4-A2-GreenspacePres.pptx**.	1	
2	Inserting, formatting Slide	Insert slide shown in Fig. 4.18 with the following specifications: g. Make Slide 2 active and insert new slide with the *Blank* layout. h. Insert WordArt text using *Pattern Fill - Gold, Accent 3, Narrow Horizontal Inner Shadow* (second column, bottom row). i. Change WordArt shape to *Wave 1* (first option in fifth row in *Warp* section of Text Effects, Transform menu). j. Change height of WordArt to 4-inches and width to 10-inches. k. Distribute the WordArt horizontally and vertically on the slide l. Display Format Background task pane. Insert a check mark in the *Hide background* graphics. Click the Preset gradients, click the *Light Gradient- Accent 3 option* (third column, first row) Close task pane.	5	
3	Inserting Slide, Formatting	Insert slide as shown in Fig. 4.19 with the following specifications: a. Make Slide 8 active and insert new slide with *Title Only* layout. b. Insert title *English/French Translations* as shown in Fig. 4.19 c. Insert text box, change font size to 28, set left tabs at 1-inch and 5.5-inch marks on horizontal ruler. Type text as shown in Fig. 4.19 in columns. Bold headings *English Name* and *French Name*. Use Symbol dialog box to insert special symbols in French names. (Use the (normal text) font at the Symbol dialog box to insert the symbols. d. If necessary, move text box so it is positioned as shown in Fig. 4.19.	4	
4	Formatting	Make the following changes in Slide 4: a. Change bulleted line spacing to 2.0. b. Set bulleted text in two columns c. Size the placeholder so four bulleted items display in each column	3	

Steps	Tasks	Criteria	Value	Score
5	Inserting and Formatting Clip Art	In Slide 5, insert a clip art image as shown in Figure 4.20 with the following specifications: a. Use the words *watering can gardening tools* to search for the image. b. Flip the image horizontally. c. Change the height of the image to 4-inches d. Display the Format Picture task pane with the Size & Properties icon selected and then change the horizontal position to 6-inches and the vertical position to 2.2-inches.	5	
6	Inserting Slide, Clip Art	In Slide 9: insert a new slide with the Title Only layout. Create the slide shown in Figure 4.21 with the following specifications: a. Insert the title *Gardening Magazines* b. Create the top shape using the *Bevel* shape. Change the height of the shape to 1.1-inches and the width to 10-inches. c. Change the font size to 32 points and then type the text in the top shape. Insert the registered Symbol dialog box with the (normal text) font selected. d. Select and then copy the shape two times. Use the guidelines and Smart Guides to help you align and position the shapes. e. Change the text in the second and third shapes to match what you see in Figure 4.21. f. Group the three shapes: apply the *Dark Green, Text 2, Lighter 60%* shape fill color, the *Olive Green, Accent 1, Darker 50%* shape outline, and the *Dark Green, Text 2, Darker 25%* text fill color.	5	
7	Inserting and formatting a Slide	Make Slide 10 active: insert a new slide with the Title Only layout. Type **Gift Certificate** as the title and then insert a screenshot with the following specifications: a. Open Word and then open the document name **GAGiftCert.docx** from the PC4 folder on your storage medium. b. Click the PowerPoint button on the Taskbar and then use the *Screen Clipping* option from the Screenshot button drop-down list to capture only the gift certificate in the Word document. c. With the gift certificate screenshot inserted in the slide, change the height to 3.5 inches and distribute the certificate horizontally and vertically on the slide. d. Make Word Active and then close Word.	5	
8-10	Running, Printing, Saving	Run presentation. Print handout with six slides horizontally per page. Save the **PC4A2GreenspacePres.pptx** presentation.	2	
		TOTAL POINTS	30	

Assessment 3: Copy a Picture from a Website to a Presentation
File: **P-C4-A2-GreenspacePres.pptx**

Steps	Tasks	Criteria	Value	Score
1-2	Using Help	With the **PC4A2GreenspacePres.pptx** presentation open, make Slide 6 active. Use Help feature to find information on copying a picture from a web page.	3	
3	Inserting Picture from the Web	Using information learned, use a search engine to search for picture from a web page, using the *Bing Image Search* text box to search for a picture of flowers on the web. Insert the picture in Slide 6. Size and move the picture so it is positioned attractively in the slide.	4	
4-6	Printing, Runing and Saving	Print only Slide 6. Run presentation. Save and close presentation as **PC4A2GreenspacePres.pptx**	3	
		TOTAL POINTS	10	

Visual Benchmark

Creating a Study Abroad Presentation
File: **P-C4-VB-RomeStudy.pptx**

Steps	Tasks	Criteria	Value	Score
1	Creating, Formatting Inserting images in a Presentation	Create presentation as illustrated in Fig. 4.22 with the following specifications: a. Apply *Quotable* design theme and choose the *Purple variant*. b. In Slide 1, increase font size for the subtitle to 36; c. In Slide 2, insert WordArt using the *Pattern Fill - Purple, Accent 1, 50% Hard Shadow – Accent 1* option. Apply the *Deflate* transform text effect. Size and position the WordArt on slide as shown in Fig. 4.22. d. Change line spacing to 2 for bulleted text in Slides 3 and 4, and change the line spacing to one-and-a-half spacing (1.5) for the bulleted text in Slide 5. e. Use the words *apartment building* to search for the clip art image in Slide 4. Change original color (dark pink) to *Purple, Accent color 1 Light*. (If clip art image is not available, select similar image.) Size and position the image as shown in Figure 4.22. f. Insert **Colosseum.jpg** in Slide 5 (located in PC4 folder). Size and position as shown in Fig. 4.22. g. In Slide 6, use Bevel shape in *Basic Shapes* section to create the shape. Change font size to 20 points for the text in the shapes. h. Make other changes to placeholders and objects so slides are similar to slides in Fig. 4.22.	14	
2	Formatting	Apply transition and sound of student's choosing to all slides.	4	

Steps	Tasks	Criteria	Value	Score
3-5	Saving, Printing, Closing	Save and close **P-C4-VB-RomeStudy**. Print as handout with six slides horizontally per page. Close **PC4-VB-RomeStudy.pptx**.	2	
		TOTAL POINTS	20	

Case Study

Part 1

File: **P-C4-CS-HFS.pptx**

Steps	Tasks	Criteria	Value	Score
1	Opening Word	Open Word and the **HFS.docx** file. Read document.	1	
2	Creating, Proofreading Presentation	Based on the information provided in the Word document, create a presentation with the following specifications: Slide 1: Include company name Honoré Financial Services and subtitle *Managing Your Money*. Slide 2: Insert *Budgeting* as WordArt. Slides 3, 4, 5: Use bulleted and numbered information. Slide 6: Create text box, set tabs, and type information in the *Managing Records* section that is set in columns. Slide 7: Create shape and insert slogan *Retirement Planning Made Easy*. Include at least one picture and one clip art in presentation. Proofread and correct errors.	9	
2	Formatting	Apply design theme of student's choosing. Add additional features to improve visual appeal.	2	
3	Formatting	Insert transition and sound to each slide. Run presentation.	2	
5	Saving, Printing	Save as **P-C4-CS-HFS.pptx**. Print handout with four slides horizontally per page.	1	
		TOTAL POINTS	15	

Part 2

File: **P-C4-CS-HFS.pptx**

Steps	Tasks	Criteria	Value	Score
1	Inserting Slide	With **P-C4-CS-HFS.pptx** open, create a slide at end of presentation. Include a shape with text inside that includes a shape with text inside that includes the information about the workshop. Student determines day, time, and location for workshop.	3	
2	Printing	Print the slide.	2	
		TOTAL POINTS	5	

Part 3

File: **P-C4-CS-HFSWorkshop.docx**

Steps	Tasks	Criteria	Value	Score
1	Opening New Word Document, Copying Shape	Open blank Word document. Copy shape from last slide and insert in Word document.	1	
2	Formatting	Change to landscape orientation. Increase size of shape. Drag shape to middle of page.	3	
3	Saving, Printing	Save Word document as **PC4CSHFSWorkshop.docx**. Print and close document.	1	
		TOTAL POINTS	5	

Part 4

File: **P-C4-CS-HFS.pptx**

Steps	Tasks	Criteria	Value	Score
1	Researching	Using the Internet, locate at least two online finance and/or budgeting resources.	1	
2	Creating Slide with Hyperlinks	Create a new slide at end of presentation with hyperlinks to the resources.	3	
3	Printing, Saving	Print slide containing hyperlinks. Save and close the **P-C4-CS-HFS.pptx** presentation.	1	
		TOTAL POINTS	5	

Benchmark PowerPoint 2013 Level 1, Unit 1 Performance Assessment

Assessing Proficiency

Assessment 1: Prepare, Format, and Enhance a Conference Presentation
File: **P-U1-A1-CSConf.pptx**

Steps	Tasks	Criteria	Value	Score
1	Creating Presentation	Create presentation with text shown in Fig. U.1. Use *Quotable* design theme. Use appropriate slide layout for each slide. Complete spell check. Proofread and correct errors.	4	
2	Formatting	Add transition and sound of student's choosing to all slides.	2	
3-4	Saving	Save presentation as **P-U1-A1-CSConf**. Run presentation.	1	
5	Find and Replace	With Slide 1 active, final all occurrences of *Area* and replace with *Market*.	1	

Steps	Tasks	Criteria	Value	Score
6	Editing	With Slide 2 active, type **Net income per common share** over *Net income*. Delete *Return on average equity*.	1	
7	Editing	With Slide 4 active, delete *Shopping*. Type **Business finance** between *Personal finance* and *Email*.	1	
8	Rearranging Slides	Rearrange slides in following order (by title): Slide 1 = CORNERSTONE SYSTEMS Slide 2 = Corporate Vision Slide 3 = Future Goals Slide 4 = Industrial Market Slide 5 = Consumer Market Slide 6 = Financial Review	2	
9	Adjusting Spacing	Increase spacing to 1.5 for bulleted text in Slides 2, 3, 5, and 6.	1	
10	Formatting	With Slide 4 active, increase spacing to 2.0 for bulleted text. Format bulleted text into two columns with three entries in each column.	2	
11-12	Saving, Printing	Save and run presentation. Print handout with six slides horizontally per page.	1	
13-16	Reusing Slides	Using Reuse Slides task pane, double-click **CSMktRpt.pptx**. Insert *Department Reports* slide below Slide 4. Insert *Services* slide below Slide 2. Close Reuse Slides task pane.	3	
17-18	Creating Custom Bullet, Inserting Clip Art	With Slide 8 active, select bulleted text, create and apply a custom bullet using a dollar sign in a complementary color. Insert a clip art image related to *money* or *finances*. Size and position clip art attractively in slide 8.	4	
19	Moving Slide	Move Slide 4 (Future Goals) to end of presentation.	1	
20	Inserting New Slide	Insert new slide with *Title and Content* layout at end of presentation with the following specifications: a. Insert *Future Goals* as title. b. Type **International market** as first bulleted item and press Enter. c. Copy *Acquisitions, Production, Technology,* and *Marketing* from Slide 8. Paste in content area of new slide below first bulleted text. d. Select bulleted text and change line spacing to 1.5.	4	
21-22	Applying Numbering	With Slide 8 active, select bulleted items and apply numbering. With Slide 9 active, select bulleted items and apply numbering. Change the beginning number to *6*.	2	

Steps	Tasks	Criteria	Value	Score
23	Creating New Slide	With Slide 9 active, create new slide with *Blank* layout with the following specifications: a. Insert picture named **Nightscape.jpg** as background picture. Hide background graphics. b. Create text box toward top of slide. Change font color to white. Increase font size to 36. Change alignment to center. c. Type **National Sales Meeting**, press Enter, type **New York City**, press Enter, and type **March 4 – 6, 2015.** d. Move and/or size text box so text is positioned centered above buildings in picture.	3	
24	Creating New Slide	With Slide 10 active, insert a new slide with *Title Only* layout. Type **Doubletree Guest Suites** as title. Insert screenshot with the following specifications: a. Open Word document named **HotelMap.docx**. b. Use *Screen Clipping* option from Screenshot button drop-down list to capture only the map in Word document. c. With map screenshot inserted in slide, apply *Sharpen: 25%* correction. Size and position map attractively on slide.	3	
25	Inserting Slide Numbers	Insert slide numbers on each slide.	1	
26	Inserting Footer	Insert footer for notes and handouts pages that prints student's first and last names.	2	
27-29	Saving, Printing	Save and run presentation. Print handout with six slides horizontally per page. Close **P-U1-A1-CSConf.pptx**.	1	
		TOTAL POINTS	40	

Assessment 2: Format and Enhance a Kraft Artworks Presentation
File: **P-U1-A2-KAPres.pptx**

Steps	Tasks	Criteria	Value	Score
1	Opening, Saving	Open **KAPres.pptx**. Save presentation as **PU1A2KAPres**.	1	
2	Typing Text, Formatting	With Slide 1 active, insert text *Kraft Artworks* as WordArt. Apply at least the following formatting: a. Change shape of WordArt. b. Change size so WordArt bills slide better. c. Change fill to a purple color. d. Apply other formatting to improve visual appeal of WordArt.	4	
3	Duplicating Slides	Duplicate Slides 2 and 3.	2	
4-5	Editing	In Slide 4, change goal number from *1* to *3*. Change goal text to *Conduct six art workshops at the Community Center.* In Slide 5, change goal number from *2* to *4*. Change goal text to *Provide recycled material to public schools for art classes.*	2	

Steps	Tasks	Criteria	Value	Score
6	Inserting Slide	With Slide 5 active, insert new slide with *Title Only* layout with the following specifications: a. Insert title *Clients*. Format, size, and position title in same manner as title in Slide 5. b. Insert text box, change font to Comic Sans MS, font size to 20, apply *Lavender, Accent 1, Darker 50% font color* and type text in columns as shown. (user determines tab settings) Select all text in text box and change line spacing to 1.5.	3	
7	Inserting Slide	With Slide 6 active, insert new slide with *Blank* layout. Hide background graphic. Create slide shown in Fig. U1.2 with the following specifications: a. Use *Explosion I* shape from *Stars and Banners* section to create first shape. b. Apply Light green shape fill color and aPPPLY *Lavender, 18 pt glow, Accent color 2* glow effect. c. With shape selected, change font to 40-point Comic Sans MS bold in Lavender, Accent 1, Darker 50% font color then type text as shown in Fig. U1.2. d. Copy shape twice. Position shapes as illustrated. e. Type appropriate text in each text box as shown in Fig. U1.2.	6	
8	Inserting Slide	With Slide 7 active, insert new slide with *Blank* layout. Hide background graphic. Create slide shown in Fig. U1.3 with the following specifications: a. Set text in two text boxes at left and right sides of slide in 54-point Comic Sans MS bold and Lavender, Accent 1, Darker 50% font color. Rotate, size, and position two text boxes as shown in Fig. U1.3 b. Use *Explosion I* shape to create shape in middle of slide. c. Apply the Light Green shape fill color, the Lavender, 18 pt glow, Accent color 2 glow effect, the Perspective Diagonal Upper Left shadow effect, the Lavender, Accent 1, Darker 50% shape outline color and the 2 ¼ points shape outline weight. d. Insert text in shape. Change font to 28-point Comic Sans MS bold, apply Lavender, Accent 1, Darker 50% font color. Change alignment to center. Change vertical alignment to middle.	4	
9	Creating Footer	Create footer on handout pages with student's first and last names and current date.	2	
10-11	Printing, Saving	Print handout with four slides horizontally per page. Save and close **P-U1-A2-KAPres.pptx**.	1	
		TOTAL POINTS	25	

Assessment 3: Create and Apply a Custom Theme to a Job Search Presentation
File: **P-U1-A3-JobSearch.pptx**

Steps	Tasks	Criteria	Value	Score
1-5	Formatting	Format a blank presentation with the following specifications: Apply the *Dividend* design theme and the green variant (third option in the Variants group). Create custom theme colors (student's first and last names): a. Change the Accent 1 color to *Brown, Accent 6, Darker 50%.* b. Change *the Accent 2 color to Olive Green, Accent 2, Darker 25%.* c. Change the *Accent 3 color to Orange, Accent 5, Darker 25%* 3. Create custom theme fonts named with student's first and last names. Change Heading font to Constantia and Body font to Cambria. Save as custom theme with student's first and last names. Close presentation without saving.	3	
6	Opening, Saving	Open **JobSearch.pptx**. Save As**P-U1-A3-JobSearch**.	1	
7	Applying Custom Theme	Apply custom theme created in Steps 1-5.	1	
8-9	Inserting Clip Art	With Slide 5 active, insert clip art related to *telephone, people,* or *Internet.* Student determines size and position of image. With Slide 6 active, insert clip art related to *clock* or *time.* Student determines size and position of image.	2	
10	Improving Visual Appeal	Improve visual appeal of Slides 2, 3, 7, 8, and 9 by increasing spacing between items and positioning text placeholders attractively in slides.	5	
11	Inserting Date and Slide Numbers	Insert current date and slide numbers on all slides in presentation. Slide numbers will appear in round circle that is part of design theme.	2	
12	Inserting Header, Footer, and Date/Page	Insert header *Job Search Seminar,* footer *Employment Strategies,* and date and page number for notes and handouts.	2	
13	Adding Speaker Note	With Slide 5 active, add speaker note *Distribute list of Internet employment site.*	2	
14-15	Formatting	Apply transition and sound of student's choosing to all slides. Save and run presentation.	2	
16-21	Printing, Saving	Print handout with six slides horizontally per page. Print Slide 5 as notes page. Change the slide size to Standard (4:3) to ensure correct fit. Scroll through slides to improve visual appearance, correct and change any needed placeholders, clip art images Save and close **P-U1-A3-JobSearch.pptx**.	2	
		TOTAL POINTS	25	

Assessment 4: Format and Enhance a Medical Plans Presentation
File: **P-U1-A4-MedicalPlans.pptx**

Steps	Tasks	Criteria	Value	Score
1	Opening, Saving	Open **MedicalPlans.pptx**. Save As **P-U1-A4-MedicalPlans**.	1	
2	Apply Theme	Apply design theme of student's choosing.	2	
3	Inserting New Slide	Insert new slide with *Blank* layout between Slides 1 and 2. Include shape with text *Medical Plans 2015 – 2016* inside shape. Student determines format, position, size of shape, and formatting of text.	3	
4	Creating Custom Bullets	Change bullets in Slides 3, 4, and 5 to custom bullets. Student determines picture or symbol.	3	
5	Inserting Clip Art	With Slide 4 active, insert clip art image related to *medicine*. Student determines color, size, and position of image.	2	
6	Formatting	With Slide 5 active, apply the following formatting: a. At beginning of *Eugene*, press Enter key twice. b. Select all bulleted text and change line spacing to 2.0. c. With bulleted text selected, format text into two columns with four entries in each column. d. Size and/or move placeholder so bulleted text displays attractively on slide.	4	
7	Formatting	Apply additional formatting or elements to improve visual appeal of slides (student decides).	2	
8	Formatting	Add transition and sound of student's choosing.	2	
9-11	Printing, Saving	Run presentation. Print handout with four slides horizontally per page. Save and close **P-U1-A4-MedicalPlans.pptx**.	1	
		TOTAL POINTS	20	

Writing Activities

Activity 1: Prepare and Format a Health Plan Presentation
File: **P-U1-Act1-KLHPlan.pptx**

Steps	Tasks	Criteria	Value	Score
1	Opening, Printing Word	Open **KLHPlan.docx** Word document. Print document.	2	
2	Creating Presentation	After reading document, create presentation highlighting main points of the plan, using bullets. Proofread and correct errors.	10	
3	Formatting	Add transition and sound of student's choosing.	2	
4	Formatting	Apply formatting and/or insert images to enhance visual appeal of presentation.	4	
5	Saving, Printing	Save As **P-U1-Act1-KLHPlan.pptx**. Run presentation. Print handouts with six slides horizontally per page.	2	
		TOTAL POINTS	20	

Activity 2: Prepare and Format a Presentation on Saving an Image as a JPG
File: **P-U1-Act2-JPGPres.pptx**

Steps	Tasks	Criteria	Value	Score
1	Using Help	Use Help feature to research how to insert a picture or clip art image. Print then read information from Help feature. Close presentation without saving.	2	
2	Creating Presentation	Based on reading information from Help, create presentation with at least three slides: title slide, slide with steps on saving an image in the JPG format, and a slide on the various file formats for saving an image..	8	
3	Formatting	Format presentation appropriately	2	
4	Opening and grouping	Open the KLHPLogo.pptx, group the image and the text, then save the grouped image as a JPG file named KLHPLogo.jpg. in the PUI folder on storage medium. Add visual appeal to presentation.	3	
5	Formatting	Add transition and sound of student's choosing.	2	
6	Saving	Save As **P-U1-Act2-JPGPres.**	1	
7	Printing	Run presentation. Print handouts with four slides horizontally per page. Close **P-U1-Act2-JPGPress.pptx**.	2	
		TOTAL POINTS	20	

Internet Research

Activity 1: Analyze a Magazine Website

File: **P-U1-TimeMag.pptx**

Steps	Tasks	Criteria	Value	Score
1	Exploring a Website	Connect to the Internet, explore *Time*® magazine at **www.time. com**, and review the following information: • Magazine sections • Type of information presented in each section • Information on how to subscribe	5	
2	Creating Presentation	Create presentation based on information found at the *Time*® magazine site. Material is presented in a clear, concise, and logical manner. Proofread and correct errors.	10	
3	Formatting	Add formatting and enhancements to presentation to make it more interesting.	4	
4	Saving, Printing, Closing	Save As **P-U1-TimeMag**. Run, print, and close presentation.	1	
		TOTAL POINTS	20	

Benchmark PowerPoint 2013 Level 1, Chapter 5

Skills Check

Assessment 1: Create and Format Tables and SmartArt in a Restaurant Presentation
File: **P-C5-A1-Dockside.pptx**

Steps	Tasks	Criteria	Value	Score
1	Opening, Saving	Open **Dockside.pptx**. Save As **P-C5-A1-Dockside.pptx**.	1	
2	Creating Table	In Slide 6 create table as shown in Fig. 5.15 with the following specifications: a. Create table with three columns and six rows. b. Type text in cells as illustrated in Fig. 5.15. c. Apply *Medium Style 1 - Accent 2* style to table. d. Table text: centered vertically, font size 20 point, font color to *Turquoise, Accent 2, Darker 50%*. e. Table height 3.7-inches; width 9-inches. f. Center text in first row. g. Center text in third column. h. Horizontally distribute the table.	6	
3	Creating Table	In Slide 4 create table as shown in Figure 5.16 with the following specifications: a. Create table with four columns and three rows. b. Change vertical alignment of table to center, change font size to 28. c. Merge cells in first column, change text direction to *Rotate all text 270°*, center alignment, font size 40, type **Lunch**. d. Merge cells in third column, change text direction to *Rotate all text 270°*, center alignment, font size 40, type **Dinner**. e. Type text as shown in Figure 5.16 f. Change table height to 3 inches. g. Change width of first and third columns to 1.2 inches. h. Change width of second and fourth columns to 2.5 inches. i. Insert *Banded Columns* in Table Style Options and remove all other options in group. j. Apply *Light Style3 - Accent 2* style to table. k. Change table text to *Light Turquoise, Background 2, Darker 75%*. l. Distribute the table horizontally on the slide.	6	
4	Creating Organizational Chart	In Slide 5 create SmartArt organizational chart as shown in Figure 5.17 with the following specifications: a. Chose *Half Circle Organizational Chart*. b. Delete second box; chart appears as illustrated in Fig. 5.17. c. Type text in in boxes as shown in Fig. 5.17. d. Change color to *Colorful Range - Accent Colors 3 to 4*. e. Apply Polished SmartArt style. f. Change the text fill color to *Dark Teal, Text 2, Darker 25%* g. Change height of organizational chart to 6.5- inches and width to 10-inches. h. Distribute the SmartArt organizational chart horizontally on the slide..	5	

Steps	Tasks	Criteria	Value	Score
5	Creating SmartArt	In Slide 1 create SmartArt diagram as shown in Fig. 5.18 with the following specifications: a. Create the SmartArt graphic with the Linear Venn option located in the Relationship group.. b. Type text in shapes as shown in Fig. 5.18. c. Change colors to *Colorful - Accent Colors*. d. Apply *Cartoon* SmartArt style. e. Change the height of the graphic to 3-inches and the width to 9-inches f. Align the SmartArt at the bottom of the slide.	5	
6	Converting Text to SmartArt	In slide 2, convert bulleted text to *Basic Matrix* SmartArt graphic as shown in Fig. 5.19 with the following specifications: a. Change colors to *Colorful - Accent Colors*. b. Apply *Cartoon* SmartArt style. c. Change height of diagram to 4.5 inches .	4	
7-8	Applying Transition	Apply a transition and sound of your choosing to all slides in the presentation. Run the presentation.	2	
9-10	Printing, Saving, Closing	Print handout with six slides horizontally per page. Save and close **P-C5-A1-Dockside.pptx**.	1	
		TOTAL POINTS	30	

Assessment 2: Create and Format Charts in a Marketing Presentation
File: **P-C5-A2-MarketingPres.pptx**

Steps	Tasks	Criteria	Value	Score
1	Opening, Saving	Open **MarketingPres.pptx**. Save As **P-C5-A2-MarketingPres**.	1	
2	Inserting Slide with Chart	With Slide 2 active, insert new slide with *Title and Content* layout. Create chart as shown in Fig. 5.20 with the following specifications: a. Type slide title as shown in Fig. 5.20. b. Create chart with *Pie in 3-D* pie chart option. c. Type text in Excel worksheet. d. Change chart layout to *Layout7*. e. Apply the Style 5 chart style. f. Move the legend to the right. g. Select the legend and then change the font size to 24 points. h. Insert date labels on the inside end. i. Select the data labels and then change the font size to 20 points.	6	
3	Printing	Print Slide 3.	1	
4	Editing Data	Edit Excel data: a. Change 47% to 42%. b. Change 10% to 15%.	2	

Steps	Tasks	Criteria	Value	Score
5	Inserting Slide with Chart	With Slide 3 active, insert new slide with *Title and Content* layout. Create chart as shown in Fig. 5.21 with the following specifications: a. Type slide title as shown in Fig. 5.21. b. Use *Line with Markers* line chart option. c. Type text in Excel worksheet. d. Apply *Style 4* chart style. e. Add primary major vertical gridlines. f. Add a data table with legend keys. g. Remove the title and remove the legend. h. Select the chart area and then change the font size to 18 points. i. Format Chart Area, specifying a *Gradient fill* of *Light Gradient – Accent 2* j. Select the Revenues series and then change the weight of the line to 4 ½ points k. Select the Expenses series and then change the weight of the line to 4 ½ points.	8	
6	Formatting	Apply transition and sound of student's choosing to each slide.	1	
7-9	Running, Printing, Saving	Run presentation. Print handout with three slides per page. Save the **P-C5-A2MarketingPres.pptx** presentation.	1	
		TOTAL POINTS	20	

Assessment 3: Create a Scenery Photo Album
File: **P-C5-A3-PhotoAlbum.pptx**

Steps	Tasks	Criteria	Value	Score
1	Creating New Photo Album	Create new photo album.	1	
2	Inserting Images in Photo Album	Insert the following images in Photo Album: *AlderSprings.jpg*, *CrookedRiver.jpg*, *Mountain.jpg*, *Ocean.jpg*, *Olympics.jpg*, *River.jpg*.	3	
3-6	Formatting	Change *Picture layout* to *1 picture with title*. Change *Frame shape* to *Simple Frame, White*. Apply *Integral* theme. Create.	4	
7	Changing Theme Colors	At presentation, click the DESIGN tab, click the fourth variant .	2	
8	Inserting Titles	Insert titles in specified slides: Slide 2 = Alder Springs, Oregon Slide 3 = Crooked River, Oregon Slide 4 = Mt. Rainier, Washington Slide 5 = Pacific Ocean, Washington Slide 6 = Olympic Mountain, Washington Slide 7 = Salmon River, Idaho Proofread and correct errors.	6	
9	Inserting Name	Slide 1, replace name following *by:* with student's first and last names.	2	

Steps	Tasks	Criteria	Value	Score
10-12	Saving, Printing, Closing	Save presentation as **P-C5-A3-PhotoAlbum**. Print handout with four slides horizontally per page. Close **P-C5-A3-PhotoAlbum.pptx**.	2	
		TOTAL POINTS	20	

Assessment 4: Create a Sales Area Chart
File: **P-C5-A4-MarketingPres.pptx**

Steps	Tasks	Criteria	Value	Score
1	Opening, Saving	Open **P-C5-A2-MarketingPres.pptx**. Save As **PC5A4MarketingPres**.	1	
2	Inserting New Slide	With Slide 4 active, insert new slide with *Title and Content* layout.	1	
3	Using Excel's Help and Creating Area Chart	Use Excel Help to learn about chart types. Create area chart with data provided.	4	
3	Formatting	Apply design, layout, and/or formatting to improve visual appeal of chart.	2	
4	Printing	Print Slide 5.	1	
5	Saving, Closing	Save and close **P-C5-A4-MarketingPres.pptx**.	1	
		TOTAL POINTS	10	

Visual Benchmark

Create and Format a Medical Center Presentation
File: **P-C5-VB-RMCPres.pptx**

Steps	Tasks	Criteria	Value	Score
1	Opening, Saving	Open **RMCPres.pptx** and Save As **PC5VBRMCPres**.	2	

Steps	Tasks	Criteria	Value	Score
2	Creating and Formatting a Presentation	Create presentation as illustrated in Fig. 5.22 with the following specifications: a. Create Slide 2 with the SmartArt Hierarchy relationship graphic; Apply the Colorful Range – Accent Colors 2 to 3 colors to the graphic. . b. Create Slide 3 with the SmartArt Basic Radial relationship graphic and apply the Colorful- Accent Colors to the graphic. c. Create Slide 4 and insert the table as shown in Slide 5. Apply the Medium Style 2 – Accent 1 table style and apply other formatting so your table looks similar to the figure in the table. d. Use the information shown in the data table to create the 3-D Clustered Column chart as shown in Slide 5. Apply formatting so your chart looks similar to the chart in the figure. Select chart and change the font size to 16 points and apply the Black, Text 1 font color. . e. Use the information shown in the legend and the data information at the outside end of each pie to create a 3-D pie chart as shown in Slide 6. Apply formatting so it looks similar to the chart in the figure. Select chart and change the font size to 16 points and apply the Black, Text 1 font color.	14	
3	Formatting	Apply transition and sound of student's choosing to all slides.	2	
4-5	Printing, Saving, Closing	Print as handout with six slides horizontally per page. Save and close **P-C5-VB-RMCPres.pptx**.	2	
		TOTAL POINTS	20	

Case Study

Part 1

File: **P-C5-CS-TECPres.pptx**

Steps	Tasks	Criteria	Value	Score
1	Opening Word	Open Word and the **TerraEnergy.docx** file. Read document.	1	

Steps	Tasks	Criteria	Value	Score
2 a-f	Creating Presentation	Based on the information provided in the Word document, create a presentation with the following specifications: a. Create Slide 1: Include company name subtitle, *Quarterly Meeting*. b. Create a slide that presents Executive Team information in table. c. Create a slide that presents the phases information in table (three columns of text in *Research and Development* section). Insert column at left side of table that includes text *New Product* rotated. d. Create a slide that presents the development team information in SmartArt organizational chart e. Create a slide that presents the revenues information in chart. Student determines type of chart. f. Create a slide that presents the United States sales information in chart. Student determines type of chart.	8	
2	Formatting	Apply design theme of student's choosing. Add additional features to improve visual appeal.	3	
3	Formatting	Insert transition and sound to each slide. Run presentation.	2	
5	Saving, Printing	Save as **P-C5-CS-TECPres.ppt**. Print handout with four slides horizontally per page.	1	
		TOTAL POINTS	15	

Part 2

File: **P-C5-CS-TECPres.pptx**

Steps	Tasks	Criteria	Value	Score
1	Inserting Slide	With **P-C5-CS-TECPres.pptx** open, create a new slide in presentation. Insert a *Funnel* SmartArt graphic. Type the following information in shapes inside funnel (turn on Text pane to type the Information in the Shapes): Updated Systems Safety Programs Market Expansion Insert *Higher Profits* below funnel. Apply formatting to SmartArt graphic to improve visual appeal.	4	
2	Printing, Saving	Print the slide. Save **P-C5-CS-TECPres.pptx**.	1	
		TOTAL POINTS	5	

Part 3

File: **P-C5-CS-TECPres.pptx**

Steps	Tasks	Criteria	Value	Score
1	Use Help Feature	Using the spreadsheet **DepartmentCosts.xlsx,** apply additional formatting to the pie chart. Save and close the workbook, exiting Excel.	1	

Steps	Tasks	Criteria	Value	Score
2	Inserting Slide	Create a new slide in **P-C5-CS-TECPres.pptx** that includes a hyperlink to the **DepartmentCosts.xlsx** workbook.	3	
3	Formatting	Run the presentation, verifying the link is correct. Review the chart in Excel. Exit Excel.		
4	Printing, Saving	Print the presentation as a handout with four slides printed horizontally per page. Save and then close **P-C5-CS-TECPres. pptx.**.	1	
		TOTAL POINTS	5	

Benchmark PowerPoint 2013 Level 1, Chapter 6

Skills Check

Assessment 1: Format a Presentation in Slide Maser View and then Save the Presentation as a Template

File: **P-C6-A1-XXXPublicationTemplate.potx**

Steps	Tasks	Criteria	Value	Score
1-5	Creating Slide Master with Formatting	At blank presentation, select Slide Master in View. Apply *Wood* theme, change theme colors to *Yellow Orange*. Select text *Click to edit Master text style*, click **HOME** tab, change font size to 24 points. Select text *Second level* in slide master and change size to 20 points.	5	
6	Inserting Image, Formatting Logo	Insert **WELogo.jpg** in master slide. Change height of logo to 0.5 inch. Drag logo to lower corner of slide master.	3	
7-8	Moving Placeholder	Click the **SLIDE MASTER**. Click first slide layout below the slide master.	1	
9	Moving Footer	Remove the check mark in the Master Layout group to remove the footer and date placeholders.	1	
10-12	Formatting	Select and delete slide layouts from third layout below slide master (*Section Header Layout*) to last layout. Preserve slide masters: click top slide master in slide thumbnail pane, click **Slide Master** tab, click *Preserve* button in Edit Master group. Close Master View button.	3	
13-14	Saving Template	Save presentation as template. Name template **XXXPublicationTemplate** (student's initials replace XXX). Close **XXXPublicationTemplate.potx**.	2	
		TOTAL POINTS	15	

Assessment 2: Use a Template to Create a Publications Presentation

File: **P-C6-A2-WEnterprises.pptx**

Steps	Tasks	Criteria	Value	Score
1-2	Opening Template, Saving Presentation	Open **XXXPublicationTemplate.potx** (student's initials replace XXX). Save presentation as **PC6A2WEnterprises**.	2	
3-4	Typing Text	In current slide, type **Worldwide Enterprises** as title. Type **Company Publications** as subtitle.	2	
5-6	Reusing Slides, Inserting Slides	Display Reuse Slides task pane, browse PC6 folder, and double-click **Publications.pptx**. Insert second, third, fourth, and fifth slides. Close task pane.	2	

Steps	Tasks	Criteria	Value	Score
7	Inserting Second Slide Master	Insert second slide master with the following specifications: In Slide Master view, click in slide thumbnail pane below bottom slide layout and change theme to Frame. Click *Frame Slide Master* thumbnail and apply the *Yellow Orange* theme colors. Apply the *Style 9 background* style.	4	
8	Deleting Slide Layouts	Select and delete slide layouts from third layout (*Section Header Layout*) below new slide master to last layout.	2	
9-10	Inserting Headers, Footers, Numbers, Dates	Insert headers, footers, slide numbers, and dates with the following specifications: a. In Header Footer dialog box, insert date to update automatically and insert slide numbers. b. In Notes and Handouts dialog box, insert date to update automatically, insert header with student's first and last names, insert footer that prints *Worldwide Enterprises*, and Apply to All. Close **Slide Master** view.	5	
11	Inserting Slide	With Slide 5 active, insert new slide using the new *Frame Title* Slide layout. Type *Worldwide Enterprises* as title and *Preparing the Company Newsletter* as subtitle.	2	
12	Inserting Text in Slides	Insert text in Slides 7 and 8 as illustrated using *Frame Title* and Content layout. Proofread and correct errors.	4	
13-14	Formatting Slides, Running presentation	Insert a transition and sound of student's choosing to all slides. Run the presentation.	4	
15	Printing, Saving and closing	Print the presentation as a handout with four slides printed horizontally per page. Save and close as **P-C6-A2-WEnterprises. pptx**.	3	
		TOTAL POINTS	30	

Assessment 3: Insert Action Buttons in a Gardening Presentation
File: **P-C6-A3-GAPres.pptx**

Steps	Tasks	Criteria	Value	Score
1	Opening, Saving	Open **GAPres.pptx**. Save As **P-C6-A3-GAPres**.	1	
2	Inserting Action Button	In Slide 1 insert action button in lower right corner of slide that displays the next slide.	1	
3	Inserting Action Button in Slide Master	In **Slide Master** view, click top slide master in slide thumbnail pane, and create an action button in lower right corner of slide that displays next slide. Close **Slide Master** view.	2	
4	Inserting Action Button	In Slide 8 create action button that display first slide in presentation.	1	
5	Linking to Presentation	In Slide 2, click *flowers* clip art image and create link to **MaintenancePres.pptx**.	1	

Steps	Tasks	Criteria	Value	Score
6	Editing Slide	In Slide 8, make the following changes: a. Delete *Better Homes and Gardens*® and replace with **Organic Gardening**®. b. Select *Organic Gardening*® and create hyperlink with text to website www.organicgardening.com.	2	
7	Running Presentation	Connect to the Internet. Run presentation beginning with Slide 1. Navigate through slide show using the action button. Display connected presentation by clicking clip art image in Slide 2. In Slide 8, click the Organic Gardening® hyperlink. Scroll through site, view a few web pages, and close web browser. Action button on last slide displays first slide. Use Esc key to end slide show.	1	
8-9	Printing, Saving	Print handout with four slides horizontally per page. Save and close **P-C6-A3-GAPres.pptx**.	1	
		TOTAL POINTS	10	

Assessment 4: Create an Action Buttons Presentation

File: **P-C6-A4-ActionButtons.pptx**

Steps	Tasks	Criteria	Value	Score
1	Creating Presentation	After experimenting with other action buttons, create presentation with the following specifications: a. First slide contains title of presentation. b. Choose four action buttons and then create one slide for each action button and include specific name as well as explanation of button. c. Apply design theme of student's choosing.	4	
2-4	Saving, Printing	Save As **P-C6-A4-ActionButtons.pptx**. Print handout with six slides horizontally per page. Close **P-C6-A4-ActionButtons.pptx**.	1	
		TOTAL POINTS	5	

Visual Benchmark

Create and Format a Company Branch Office Presentation

File: **P-C6-VB-WEClearwater.pptx**

Steps	Tasks	Criteria	Value	Score
1	Creating Presentation	Create presentation as illustrated in Fig. 6.3 with the following specifications: a. Apply *Parallax* design theme, the *gray/orange variant*, the *Arial Black Arial* theme fonts and the *Style 1 background* style. b. In Slide 1, delete the placeholder and insert **WELogo.jpg**. Size and position as shown in figure. Insert Forward or Next action button in lower right corner of slide as shown in figure. c. Display presentation in Slide Master View. Click top slide master thumbnail. Position logo in lower left corner of slide as shown in Fig. 6.3. Click to edit Master Title style text, click **HOME** tab, and change font color to *Orange, Accent 1, Darker 25%*. Insert Forward or Next action button in lower right corner of slide master as shown in figure. Close Slide Master View. d. In Slide 4, create *3-D clustered column* chart as shown in figure. e. In Slide 5, insert Information action button that links to website www.clearwaterfl.com/gov. Size and position as shown. f. In Slide 6, insert clip art image of hospital (use the search words *hospital* and *ambulance*) Change clip art color to *Brightness: -20% Contrast: +20%* Size and position as shown. g. Change line spacing in slides 5 and 6 similar to slides in Fig. 6.3.	12	
2	Formatting	Apply transition and sound of student's choosing to all slides.	2	
3-6	Saving, Printing, Closing	Save As **P-C6-VB-WEClearwater**. Run presentation. Print as handout with six slides horizontally per page. Close **PC6VBWEClearwater.pptx**.	1	
		TOTAL POINTS	15	

Case Study

Part 1

File: **AnchorTemplate.potx**

Steps	Tasks	Criteria	Value	Score
1	Creating Template	Create presentation template with attractive formatting including: design theme, theme colors, theme fonts, and clip art image of anchor in lower left corner of most slides.	6	
2	Formatting	Apply other formatting and/or design elements to increase appeal of presentation.	3	
3	Saving	Save presentation as **XXXAnchorTemplate.potx** on storage medium. XXX being student's initials. Close template	1	
		TOTAL POINTS	10	

Part 2

File: **P-C6-CS-AnchorEmp.pptx**

Steps	Tasks	Criteria	Value	Score
1	Opening Word	Open Word document **AnchorNewEmployees.docx** and read contents. Create presentation using information in document and use the **XXXAnchorTemplate.potx** template.	10	
2	Saving	Save As **P-C6-CS-AnchorEmp.pptx**.	1	
3	Formatting	Apply transition and sound of student's choosing to all slides.	3	
4	Printing, Closing	Print as handouts. Close presentation.	1	
		TOTAL POINTS	15	

Part 3

File: **P-C6-CS-AnchorGuidelines.pptx**

Steps	Tasks	Criteria	Value	Score
1	Opening Word	Open Word document **AnchorGuidelines.docx** and read contents. Create presentation using information in document and use the **XXXAnchorTemplate.potx** template. Proofread and correct errors.	10	
2	Saving	Save As **P-C6-CS-AnchorGuidelines.pptx**.	1	
3	Formatting	Apply transition and sound of student's choosing to all slides.	3	
4	Printing, Closing	Print as handouts. Close presentation.	1	
		TOTAL POINTS	15	

Part 4

File: **P-C6-CS-AnchorEmp.pptx**

Steps	Tasks	Criteria	Value	Score
1	Creating New Slide with Hyperlink to Excel	Open **P-C6-CS-AnchorEmp.pptx**. Create new slide that contains hyperlink to Excel workbook, **ACClassifications.xlsx**. Run presentation, link to Excel chart, continue running remaining slides.	4	
2, 3	Printing, Saving	Print only the new slide. Save and close **P-C6-CS-AnchorEmp.pptx**.	1	
		TOTAL POINTS	5	

Part 5
File: **P-C6-CS-AnchorGuidelines.pptx**

Steps	Tasks	Criteria	Value	Score
1	Creating New Slide with Hyperlink to Word	Create new slide in **P-C6-CS-AnchorGuidelines.pptx** that includes action button to link to Word document named Anchor**ComputerGuidelines.docx.**	3	
2	Inserting Action Buttons	Insert other action buttons navigating presentation. Run presentation, link to Word document, continue running slides remaining slides.	1	
3	Printing, Saving	Print only the new slide. Save and close **P-C6-CS-AnchorGuidelines.pptx.**	1	
		TOTAL POINTS	5	

Benchmark PowerPoint 2013 Level 1, Chapter 7

Skills Check

Assessment 1: Apply Animation Effects to a Travel Presentation
File: **P-C7-A1-FCTCruise.pptx**

Steps	Tasks	Criteria	Value	Score
1	Opening, Saving	Open **FCTCruise.pptx**. Save As **PC7A1FCTCruise.**	1	
2-3	Applying Animation	On Slide 1, click company logo and apply *Fade* animation. Apply *Fly In* animation to subtitle *Vacation Cruise.*	2	
4	Applying Animation to Slide Master	Display Slide Master view, click top slide master layout (Japanese Waves Slide Master), apply *Fade* animation to title style, and close Slide Master view.	1	
5	Applying Animation	Make Slide 2 active and apply the following: *a-b:* Click in the bulleted text and apply the *Wipe entrance* animation. c. Change the direction to *From Left.* d. Click in the bulleted text. e. Double-click the Animation Painter button. f. Make Slide 3 active and then click in the bulleted text. g. Make Slide 4 active and click in bulleted text. h. Make Slide 5 active and click in bulleted text. i. Click on Animation Painter button to deactivate.	2	

Steps	Tasks	Criteria	Value	Score
6	Inserting Trigger	Make Slide 3 active and insert trigger by completing the following: a. Click banner that displays toward bottom of slide and apply *Wipe* animation and change direction to *From Left*. b. Display Animation Pane. c. Click *Horizontal Scroll* in the Animation Pane. d. Click Trigger button, point to *On Click of*, and click *Content Placeholder 2* at side menu. e. Close Animation Pane.	3	
7-8	Running and Saving	Run presentation. When third bulleted item in Slide 3 displays, click bulleted item to trigger display of banner. Save and close **P-C7-A1-FCTCruise.pptx**.	1	
		TOTAL POINTS	10	

Assessment 2: Apply Animation Effects to an Employee Orientation Presentation
File: **P-C7-A2-GEOrientation.pptx**

Steps	Tasks	Criteria	Value	Score
1	Opening, Saving	Open **GEOrientation.pptx**. Save presentation as **PC7A2GEOrientation**.	1	
2	Applying Animation	With Slide 2 active, apply the following animations to SmartArt graphic: a. Apply *Blinds* entrance animation effect. b. Change SmartArt animation to *One by One* and change direction to *Vertical*.	2	
3	Applying Animation to Organizational Chart	With Slide 3 active, apply the following animations to organizational chart: a. Apply *Blinds* entrance animation effect. b. Change SmartArt animation to *Level at Once*.	2	
4	Applying Animation to Bulleted Text	With Slide 4 active, apply the following animations to bulleted text: a. Apply *Zoom* entrance animation effect. b. In Animation Pane, set text to dim after animation to a dark blue color.	2	
5	Applying Animation to Clip Art	With Slide 4 active, apply the following animations to clip art image: a. Apply *Spin* emphasis animation effect. b. Set amount of spin for clip art image to *Two Spins* and change duration to *01.00*. c. Change the *Start* option to *With Previous*. d. Reorder the items in the Animation Pane so the clip art displays first when running the presentation.	2	
6	Applying Animation to SmartArt Graphic	With Slide 5 active, select SmartArt graphic and apply animation effect so elements in SmartArt Graphic fade in one by one.	1	

Steps	Tasks	Criteria	Value	Score
7	Applying Animation Effect to Images	With Slide 6 active, apply the following animation effects to images with the following specifications: a. Apply *Fly Out* exit animation effect to *Free Education* gift package, change direction to *To Right*, and change duration to *00.25*. b. Apply *Shape* entrance animation effect to diploma/books clip art image, change duration to *01.00*. c. Move *Free Education* gift package book so bulleted text appears, apply *Grow & Turn* entrance animation effect to bulleted text, and move gift package back to original location. d. Apply *Fly Out* exit animation effect to *Free Toys and Fitness* gift package, change direction to *To Left*, and change duration to *00.25*. e. Apply *Shape* entrance animation effect to notebook computer clip art image and change duration to *01.00* f. Move *Free Toys and Fitness* gift package so bulleted text displays, apply *Grow & Turn* entrance animation effect to bulleted text, and move gift package back to original location. g. Close the Animation pane.	4	
8-9	Running, Saving	Make Slide 1 active and run presentation. Save **P-C7-A2-GEOrientation.pptx**.	1	
10	Applying Animation to Slide Master	Display presentation in **Slide Master** view, click top slide master layout in Slide thumbnail pane, apply *entrance* animation effect of student's choosing to title, and close Slide Master view.	2	
11	Applying Animation	With Slide 1 active, apply the following animation effects: a. Draw motion path (using Custom Path option) so globe clip art image circles around slide and returns back to original location. b. Apply *Spiral In* entrance animation to *New Employee Orientation* placeholder.	2	
12-14	Running, Printing, Saving	Run presentation. Print handout with nine slides horizontally per page. Save and close **P-C7-A2-GEOrientation.pptx**.	1	
		TOTAL POINTS	20	

Assessment 3: Apply Animation Effect, Video, and Audio to a Job Search Presentation
File: **P-C7-A3-JobSearch.pptx**

Steps	Tasks	Criteria	Value	Score
1	Opening, Saving	Open **JobSearch.pptx**. Save As **P-C7-A3-JobSearch**.	1	
2-3	Applying Design Theme, Inserting Clip Art Images	Apply *Wisp* design theme and the *blue-colored variant* (third thumbnail) to presentation. Add appropriate clip art images to at least two slides.	3	

Steps	Tasks	Criteria	Value	Score
4	Inserting Video File	With Slide 10 active, insert video file name **Flight.mov** from PC7 folder. Make the following changes to video: a. Change height to 5 inches (Video Tools Format). b. Play video automatically (Video Tools Playback), play video in full screen, and hide video when not playing. c. Trim approximately the first nine seconds from start of video (Trim Video). Close dialog box.	3	
6	Compress Video File	Compress the video file.	3	
5, 7	Inserting, Running Audio File	With Slide 10 active, insert **AudioFile-03.mid** audio file, play automatically, loop until stopped, and hide when running presentation. Run the presentation. After listening to music end the presentation.	3	
8	Printing	Print only Slide 10.	1	
9-11	Creating Custom Show	Create custom show named *Interview* that contains Slides 1, 3, 6, 7, and 9. Run Interview custom show. Print handout of *Interview* custom show with all slides printed horizontally on one page.	2	
12	Editing	Remove Slide 2 of *Interview* custom show.	2	
13-14	Printing, Saving	Print handout of Interview custom show with all slides printed horizontally on one page. Save and close **P-C7-A3-JobSearch.pptx**.	2	
		TOTAL POINTS	20	

Assessment 4: Insert an Audio Clip from the Clip Art Task Pane
File: P-C7-A4-JamaicaTour.pptx

Steps	Tasks	Criteria	Value	Score
1	Opening, Saving	Open **JamaicaTour.pptx**. Save As **P-C7-A4-JamaicaTour**.	1	
2-3	Inserting Clip Art Audio	INSERT Online Audio, and select *Jamaica Bounce* (1 or 2). If not available, select another audio file such as *Rainforest* music, *African song* or a different audio of student's choosing.	1	
4-7	Changing Settings, Running	Set audio file to play automatically across all slides and hide when running presentation. Display the TRANSITIONS tab, and specify that each slide automatically advances after five seconds. Set presentation to run on endless loop. Run presentation.	2	
8-9	Printing, Saving	Print handout with six slides horizontally per page. Save and close **P-C7-A4-JamaicaTour.pptx**.	1	
		TOTAL POINTS	5	

Visual Benchmark

Create and Format a Medical Center Presentation

File: **P-C7-VB-RMCPres.pptx**

Steps	Tasks	Criteria	Value	Score
1	Opening, Saving	Open **RMCPres.pptx**. Save As **P-C7-VB-RMCPres**.	1	
2	Creating Presentation	Create presentation as illustrated in Fig. 7.6 with the following specifications: a. Search for clip art image *caduceus healthcare*. Size and position the clip art as shown in the figure. b. Create SmartArt in Slide 3 using *Staggered Process* diagram and apply *Colorful* Range – Accent Colors 4 to 5 option to diagram. c. Use information shown in legend and data information above bars to create *Clustered Column* chart as shown in Slide 4. Increase the text size of all elements on the chart to 16 points. d. Use *Heart* shape to create hearts in Slide 5. Apply the *Subtle Effect – Red, Accent 1 shape* style and change the shape outline weight to 4 ½ pt for all three shapes. e. Use *Frame* shape to create shape in Slide 6.	3	
3-4	Applying Animation, running	Apply animation effect to items in slides with the following specifications: a. Display Slide Master view, click top slide master layout, (Medical Health 16x9 Slide Master) and apply *Float In* animation to title style, and close Slide Master view. b. With Slide 1 active, apply animation of student's choosing to subtitle. c. With Slide 2 active, apply animation effect of student's choosing to clip art image and apply animation effect of student's choosing to bulleted text. d. With Slide 3 active, apply animation effect of student's choosing to SmartArt and specify sequence of *One by One*. e. With Slide 4 active, apply an animation effect of your choosing to the chart, and then specify a sequence of *By Category*. f. With Slide 5 active, apply *Shape* entrance animation effect to heart at left side of slide. Use Add Animation button to apply *Pulse* emphasis animation effect. Use Animation Painter to apply entrance and emphasis animation effect to middle heart and heart at right side of slide. g. With Slide 6 active, insert **AudioFile-04.mid** audio file, set to play automatically, loop until stopped, and hide when running presentation. Run presentation.	10	
5-6	Printing, Saving	Print as handout with six slides horizontally per page. Save and close **PC7VBRMCPres.pptx**.	1	
		TOTAL POINTS	15	

Case Study

Part 1

File: **P-C7-CS-PCBuyGuide.pptx**

Steps	Tasks	Criteria	Value	Score
1	Opening Word	Open Word document **PCBuyGuide.docx**. Read document to prepare for training presentation.	1	
2	Creating Presentation	Create slide presentation for contract employees on how to purchase a personal computer. Keep slides uncluttered and easy to read. Insert clip art or other images in some slides. Insert custom animation effects to each slide. Run presentation and make any necessary changes to animation effects. Proofread and correct errors.	8	
3	Saving, Printing	Save presentation as **P-C7-CS-PCBuyGuide.** Print presentation as handout.	1	
		TOTAL POINTS	10	

Part 2

File: **P-C7-CS-PCBuyGuide.pptx**

Steps	Tasks	Criteria	Value	Score
1	Creating Custom Show	With **P-C7-CS-PCBuyGuide.pptx** open, create custom show. Student determines name of show.	3	
2	Selecting Slides	Only use slides pertaining to selecting hardware components. Run custom show.	6	
3	Printing, Saving	Print custom show. Save **P-C7-CS-PCBuyGuide.pptx**.	1	
		TOTAL POINTS	10	

Part 3

File: **P-C7-CS-PCBuyGuide.pptx**

Steps	Tasks	Criteria	Value	Score
1	Searching the Internet	Use search engine to find free audio files. Search for *"free audio files for PowerPoint"* or *"free audio clips for PowerPoint."* Check to be sure audio file can be downloaded and used without violating copyright laws.	4	
2	Downloading	Download audio file.	1	
3	Inserting Audio File	Insert audio file in last slide of presentation.	2	
4	Changing Settings	Set up audio file to play after all elements display on slide.	2	
5	Saving, Closing	Save **P-C7-CS-PCBuyGuide.pptx**. Close presentation.	1	
		TOTAL POINTS	10	

Benchmark PowerPoint 2013 Level 1, Chapter 8

Skills Check

Assessment 1: Copy Word and Excel Data into a Sales Conference Presentation
File: **P-C7-A1-FCTCruise.pptx**

Steps	Tasks	Criteria	Value	Score
1	Opening, Saving	Open **NWPres.pptx**. Save As **PC8A1NWPres**.	1	
2	Opening Excel, Copying	With Slide 2 active, complete the following steps: a. Open Excel and **SalesProj.xlsx** workbook located in PC8 folder. b. Copy chart and paste into Slide 2. c. Resize chart to fill most of slide below title. d. Close workbook and exit Excel.	4	
3	Drawing Text Box, Copying Word Text	With Slide 4 active, complete the following steps: a. Draw textbox in slide. b. Open Word and open **HerbRemedies.docx**. c. Copy first three terms and paragraph below each term. Paste in text box in Slide 4. d. Move and/or resize the placeholder so it fills most of the slide below the title.	5	
4-5	Drawing Text Box, Copying Word Text	With Slide 5 active, complete the following steps: a. Draw text box in slide. b. Make **HerbRemedies.docx** active. c. Copy last two terms and paragraph below each term. Paste in text box in Slide 5. d. Move and/or size the text box so it fills most of the slide below the title. e. With Word active, close **HerbRemedies.docx**, and exit Word.	4	
6-7	Applying Animation	With PowerPoint active, apply animation effects to each item on each slide. Run presentation.	3	
8-9	Saving and Printing	Save **P-C8-A1-NWPres.pptx**. Print handout with six slides horizontally per page.	1	
10-13	Exporting to Word, Saving, Printing, Closing	Export presentation to Word document that prints blank lines next to slides. Save As **P-C8-A1-NWPresHandout.docx**. Print and close **P-C8-A1-NWPresHandout.docx**, then exit Word. Close **P-C8-A1-NWPres.pptx**.	2	
		TOTAL POINTS	20	

Assessment 2: Copy and Link Word and Excel Data into a Communications Presentation
File: **P-C7-A2-GEOrientation.pptx**

Steps	Tasks	Criteria	Value	Score
1	Opening, Saving	Open **CommPres.pptx**. Save presentation as **PC8A2CommPres**.	1	

Steps	Tasks	Criteria	Value	Score
2-5	Opening Word, Copying Table, Resizing	Open Word and **VerbalSkills.docx** located in PC8 folder. Copy table and embed it using Paste Special and Microsoft Word Document Object in Slide 5. Resize table to fill slide. Make Word active, close **VerbalSkills.docx**, and exit Word.	3	
6-8	Opening Excel, Copying Chart, Resizing, Saving	Open Excel and **NVCues.xlsx**. Copy chart and link to Slide 6. Resize chart to fill most of slide below title. Save and close **P-C8-A2-CommPres.pptx**.	3	
9-10	Editing, Saving	Make the following changes to chart in **NVCues.xlsx**: Change the amount in B2 from 35% to 38%. Change the amount in B3 from 25% to 22%. Save and close **NVCues.xlsx** and exit Excel.	2	
11-15	Opening File, Inserting Comment	Open **P-C8-A2-CommPres.pptx** and click Update Links. With Slide 2 active, insert the following comment after second bulleted item: **Ask Lauren to provide a specific communication example.** With Slide 4 active, insert the following comment after third bulleted item: **Insert a link here to the writing presentation prepared by Sylvia.** With Slide 8 active, insert the following comment after the third bulleted item: **Distribute evaluation forms to audience.** Run presentation. Proofread and correct errors.	6	
16	Saving, Printing	Save presentation. Print handout with four slides horizontally per page. Be sure comments print.	1	
17-20	Running Document Inspector and Accessibility Checker	Run Document Inspector and remove comments. Run Accessibility Checker. Create the following alt text for chart in Slide 6 with the title *Top Five Nonverbal Cues* and description *Eye contact, 38%; Smiling 22%; Posture, 15%; Position, 15%; Gestures, 10%.* Close Format Object Task pane and the Accessibility Checker task pane. Save and close **P-C8-A2-CommPres.pptx**.	4	
		TOTAL POINTS	20	

Assessment 3: Save a Sales Conference Presentation in Various Formats
File: **P-C8-A3-NWPres-2003 format.ppt, P-C8-A3-Herbs.docx, JPG files, PDF file**

Steps	Tasks	Criteria	Value	Score
1-2	Opening, Saving	Open **P-C8-A1-NWPres.pptx**. Save in PowerPoint 97-2003 Presentation and Save As **P-C8-A3-NWPres-2003format**. Close **P-C8-A3-NWPres-2003format.ppt**.	2	
2-4	Opening, Saving, Closing	Open **P-C8-A1-NWPres.pptx**. Save each slide as a **JPEG** image file. Close **P-C8-A1-NWPres.pptx** without saving changes.	3	

Steps	Tasks	Criteria	Value	Score
5	Inserting Slides in Word Document	Open a blank Word document and complete the following steps: a. Change font to Century Gothic, change font size to 24 point, change alignment to center, and type **Nature's Way**. b. Press Enter and insert **Slide4.JPG slide**. c. Change height of slide to 2.8-inches. d. Press Ctrl + End, press Enter, and insert **Slide5.JPG slide**. e Change height of slide to 2.8-inches. f. Save Word document as **P-C8-A3-Herbs**. g. Print and close **P-C8-A3-Herbs.docx**, then exit Word.	4	
6-7	Saving as PDF File	Open **P-C8-A1-NWPres.pptx** and save in PDF file format. When presentation opens in Adobe Reader, scroll through presentation and close Adobe Reader. Close **P-C8-A1-NWPres.pptx**.	3	
8	Capturing and Inserting Image	Capture image of the Open dialog box and insert image in PowerPoint slide.	1	
9-10	Printing, Closing	Print slide as full page slide. Close presentation without saving.	2	
		TOTAL POINTS	15	

Assessment 4: Download and Fill in an Award Certificate
File: **P-C8-A4-Certificate.pptx**

Steps	Tasks	Criteria	Value	Score
1	Creating Certificate	Create certificate shown in Fig. 8.7 with the following specifications: a. Display the New Backstage area, click in the Search text box, type *Award certificate* option, Download the *Excellence Award (with eagle)* template. b. Type company name as shown in Fig. 8.7, replace *Student Name* with student's name, type current date in place of *Date*, type name and title of *president/CEO* as shown in Fig. 8.7	4	
2-3	Saving, Printing	Save certificate as **P-C8-A4-Certificate**. Print and close **P-C8-A4-Certificate.pptx**.	1	
		TOTAL POINTS	5	

Visual Benchmark

1: Create JPEG Image Files and Create a Word Document
File: **P-C8-VB1-FCTCovers.docx**

Steps	Tasks	Criteria	Value	Score
1	Opening, Saving JPEG Format	Open **FCTTours.pptx**. Save all slides in presentation in JPEG graphic format. Close **FCTTours.pptx** without saving changes.	1	

Steps	Tasks	Criteria	Value	Score
2	Creating Word Document	At blank Word document, create document shown in Fig. 8.8 with the following specifications: a. Set two lines of text in *24-point Calibri bold*. b. Insert each slide and change height of each slide to 2.5-inches, change text wrapping to *Tight*, and size and position the slides as shown in Fig. 8.8.	3	
3-4	Saving, Printing	Save completed Word document as **PC8VB1FCTCovers**. Print and close **PC8VB1FCTCovers.docx**.	1	
		TOTAL POINTS	5	

2: Create a Travel Company Presentation
File: **P-C8-VB2-FCTQtrlyMtgPres.pptx**

Steps	Tasks	Criteria	Value	Score
1	Creating Presentation	Create presentation shown in Fig. 8.9 with the following specifications: a. Download design template named *Photo journal design template*. b. Delete all slides. c. At blank presentation, use **FCTQtrlyMtg.docx** Word outline to create slides in presentation. d. Insert a new slide at the beginning of presentation and insert the FCTLogo.jpg image. (see first slide in Fig 8.9) Make white background in logo transparent. Size and position logo as shown in Fig. 8.9. e. With Slide 5 active, change layout to *Title Only*, copy and link Excel chart in **Bookings.xlsx** to slide. Size and position chart as shown in Fig. 8.9. Close Excel.	8	
2-4	Saving, Printing, Closing	Save presentation as **P-C8-VB2-FCTQtrlyMtgPres**. Print handout with six slides horizontally per page. Close as **P-C8-VB2-FCTQtrlyMtgPres.pptx**.	1	
5-6	Editing Excel	Open **Bookings.xlsx** and make changes to data as indicated. Save and close **Bookings.xlsx** and exit Excel.	3	
7	Updating Links	Open **P-C8-VB2-FCTQtrlyMtgPres.pptx**. Update links.	2	
8-9	Printing, Saving	Print handout with six slides horizontally per page. Save and close **P-C8-VB2-FCTQtrlyMtgPres.pptx**.	1	
		TOTAL POINTS	15	

Case Study

Part 1
File: **RMFMLogo.pptx**

Steps	Tasks	Criteria	Value	Score
1	Saving JPEG Image	Open **RMFMLogo.pptx**. Save slide as JPEG graphic image.	2	
		TOTAL POINTS	2	

Part 2
File: **P-C8-CS-RMFMDiseases.pptx**

Steps	Tasks	Criteria	Value	Score
1	Opening Word Document	Open **ChildDiseases.docx**. Read information in document. Use the information to create a presentation.	2	
2	Creating and Formatting Slides	a. Open the **RMFMDesign.pptx** and save as **P-C8-CS-RMFMDiseases.** b. Change layout of first slide to *Title Only*, type appropriate title. c. Insert **RMFMLogo.jpg** in first slide. Set *Transparent Color* option to the background of the logo image. Size and position logo attractively on slide. d. Create additional slides based on information in **ChildDiseases.docx**. e. Proofread and correct errors. f. Apply additional enhancements to improve presentation. g. Run presentation.	10	
3	Saving, Printing, Closing	Save presentation as **P-C8-CS-RMFMDiseases**. Print handout with six slides horizontally per page. Close presentation.	1	
		TOTAL POINTS	13	

Part 3
File: **P-C8-CS-RMFMClasses.pptx**

Steps	Tasks	Criteria	Value	Score
1	Importing Outline	Open **RMFMDesign.pptx** and save and name it **P-C8CS-RMFClasses.** Import **RMFMOutline.docx** into PowerPoint presentation.	2	

Steps	Tasks	Criteria	Value	Score
2	Editing	a. Create first slide with *Title Only* layout, insert **RMFMLogo.jpg** graphic image, size and position logo similar to first slide in previous presentation **PC8CSRMFMDiseases.pptx**. Insert the title *Education and Training* in the title placeholder. b. Change layout to *Title Only* for *Community Contacts* slide. Copy table from **RMFMContacts.docx** and paste into *Community Contacts* slide. Increase size of table to better fill slide. c. Change layout to *Title Only* for *Current Enrollment* slide. Copy chart from **RMFMEnroll.xlsx**. Link to *Current Enrollment* slide. d. Apply additional enhancements to improve presentation.	10	
3	Saving, Printing, Closing	Run presentation. Save presentation as **P-C8-CS-RMFMClasses**. Print handout with six slides horizontally per page. Close presentation.	2	
4	Updating Excel Data	Open **RMFMEnroll.xlsx**. Change to following numbers: 46 to 52, 38 to 40, 24 to 27. Save and close workbook.	3	
5	Updating Links	Open **P-C8-CS-RMFMClasses.pptx** and update links.	2	
6	Printing, Closing	Print only *Current Enrollment* slide. Close presentation.	1	
		TOTAL POINTS	20	

Part 4

File: **RMFMLogo.pptx**

Steps	Tasks	Criteria	Value	Score
1	Researching Information	Using the Internet, search for information on measles including symptoms, complications, transmission, and prevention.	4	
2	Inserting Slides	Open **P-C8-Cs-RMFMDiseases.pptx** presentation. Create new slides with information obtained from the Internet. Proofread and correct errors.	10	
3-4	Running, Printing	Run presentation. Print only new slides. Save and close presentation.	1	
		TOTAL POINTS	15	

Benchmark PowerPoint 2013 Level 1, Unit 2
Performance Assessment

Assessing Proficiency

Assessment 1: Save and Insert a Slide in JPEG Format, Format a Slide Master, Create a Table and SmartArt Graphics, and Insert Comments

File: **P-U2-A1-GreenDesignPres.pptx**

Steps	Tasks	Criteria	Value	Score
1-2	Opening, Saving	Open **GreenDesignLogo.pptx**. Save only slide in presentation as a JPEG image. Close **GreenDesignLogo.pptx**. Open **GreenDesignPres.pptx**. Save As**P-U2-A1-GreenDesignPres.**	1	
3	Formatting Slide Master	Make the following changes in Slide Master view: a. Click top slide master thumbnail. b. Select *Click to Edit Master Text Styles* and change font color to *Tan, Background 2, Darker 75%* (third column, fifth row) and change the font size to *28 points*.. c. Select the text *Second level*, apply the *Green, Accent 1 font color* (fifth column, first row), and then change the font size to *24 points*. d. Close Slide Master view.	3	
4	Formatting	With Slide 1 active, make the following changes: a. Insert **GreenDesignLogo.jpg** graphic image. b. Set transparent color for logo background (white background). c. Size and position logo in the white space in the upper right corner of the slide above the water image.	2	
5	Entering Data in Table, Formatting	With Slide 6 active, use data provided and insert in table. Student determines formatting of table and formatting of data in table.	4	
6	SmartArt Organizational Chart	With Slide 7 active, use data from Figure U2.1 in a SmartArt organizational chart. Student determines organization and formatting of chart.	4	
7	Column Chart	With Slide 5 active, use data provided to create bar chart. Delete chart title and chart legend. Student determines formatting and layout.	4	
8	SmartArt Diagram	With Slide 8 active, insert SmartArt diagram using *Repeating Bending Process* diagram. Use information provided in slides from left to right. Students determine design and formatting of SmartArt graphic.	4	
9-10	Improving Visual Appeal	Check each slide and make necessary changes to improve visual appeal of slides. With Slide 1 active, run presentation.	2	
11	Inserting Comment	With Slide 3 active, insert the comment type **Check with Marilyn about adding River View Mall to this list** (click immediately right of slide title).	2	
12	Inserting Comment	With Slide 4 active, insert the comment **What happened to the plans to open an office in Sydney?** (click immediately right of word *Australia*).	2	

Steps	Tasks	Criteria	Value	Score
13-14	Printing, Saving	Print handout with four slides horizontally per page. Make sure comments print. Save and close **P-U2-A1-GreenDesignPres.pptx**.	2	
		TOTAL POINTS	30	

Assessment 2: Copy and Paste Data between Programs and Insert Action Buttons in a Travel Presentation

File: **P-U2-A2-NortonTravelPres.pptx**

Steps	Tasks	Criteria	Value	Score
1	Opening, Saving	Open **NortonTravel.pptx**. Save presentation as **PU2A2NortonTravelPres.pptx**.	1	
2	Inserting New Slide	With Slide 4 active, create a new Slide 5 with *Title Only layout*. Include the following specifications: a. Insert title *Extreme Adventures*. b. Open Word and open **NTExtremeAdventures.docx**. c. Display Clipboard task pane. Be sure task pane is empty. d. Select and copy *Small Groups* and paragraph below it including the blank line. e. Select and copy *Comprehensive Itineraries* and paragraph below it including the blank line. f. Select and copy *Custom Groups* and paragraph below it, including the blank line. g. Select and copy *Accommodations*, the paragraph below it including the blank line h. Display **PU2A2NortonTravelPres.pptx**. i. Draw a text box below the title that is approximately 10 inches wide. j. Turn on display of Clipboard task pane. k. Paste *Comprehensive Itineraries* item in text box. l. Paste *Small Groups* item in text box. m. Paste *Accommodations* item in the text box. n. Clear and close Clipboard. o. Make **NTExtremeAdventures.docx** active. Close Clipboard task pane. Close Document and close Word.	7	
3	Inserting Action Button	Make Slide 1 active and insert action button with the following specifications: a. Use *Action Button: Forward or Next* option to draw button. b. Draw button in lower right corner of slide, approximately *one-half inch* in size. c. Apply the *Subtle Effect – Aqua, Accent 2 shape style*.	4	
4-5	Slide Master	Display presentation in Slide Master view and make the following changes: a. Click top slide master thumbnail. b. Insert action button in lower right corner of slide with same specifications as completed in Step 3. c. Close Slide Master view. Run presentation using action buttons to advance slides.	4	

Steps	Tasks	Criteria	Value	Score
6	Creating footer	Create footer that prints student's first and last names at bottom of each slide. Create footer for handouts that prints presentation title *2016 Adventure Packages*. Insert date in upper right corner.	3	
7-8	Printing, Saving	Print handout with six slides horizontally per page. Save and close **P-U2-A2-NortonTravelPres.pptx**.	1	
		TOTAL POINTS	20	

Assessment 3: Save a Template Presentation and Copy, Embed, and Link Objects between Programs

File: **P-U2-A3-GSMtg.pptx**

Steps	Tasks	Criteria	Value	Score
1-2	Formatting Slide Master	Open **GSTemplate.pptx**. Display the presentation in Slide Master view, insert **GSLogo.jpg** in top slide master thumbnail, change the height of the logo to one inch, and drag the logo to the lower right corner of the slide master. Close Slide Master view.	4	
3-4	Saving	Save presentation as template in Custom Office Templates folder and name the presentation **XXXGSTemplate** (replace XXX with student's initials). Close **XXXGSTemplate.potx**.	1	
5-6	Opening, Saving	Open **XXXGSTemplate.potx**. Save presentation as **P-U2-A3-GSMtg**.	2	
7	Formatting	Format first slide with the following specifications: a. Change to *Blank* layout. b. Use WordArt to create text *Global Systems*. Student determines shape and formatting.	5	
8	Creating Slide	Create second slide with the following specifications: a. Choose *Title Slide* layout. b. Type **2016 Sales Meeting** as title. c. Type **European Division** as subtitle	2	
9	Creating Slide	Create third slide with the following specifications: a. *Title Only* layout. b. Title: **Regional Sales** c. Open Excel and **GSWorkbook01.xlsx**. d. Select cells A1 through D5. Copy, embed the cells in "Slide 3 as a Microsoft Excel Worksheet Object". e. Increase the size of the cells for appropriate fit.	2	
10	Creating Slide	Create fourth slide with the following specifications: a. *Title and Content* layout. b. Title **Company Goals**. c. Type four bulleted items as shown. (Increase product sales by 15 percent, Open a branch office in Spain, Hire one manager and two additional account managers, Decrease production costs by 6 percent)	2	

Steps	Tasks	Criteria	Value	Score
11	Creating Slide	Create fifth slide with the following specifications: a. *Title and Content* layout. b. Title **Hiring Timeline**. c. Create table with two columns and five rows and type text as shown. Student determines formatting.	2	
12-13	Creating Slide	Create sixth slide with the following specifications: a. *Title Only* layout. b. Title **Production Expenses**. c. Make Excel active and then close **GSWorkbook01.xlsx**. d. Open **GSWorkbook02.xlsx**. e. Save workbook as **GSExpensesWorkbook.xlsx**. f. Copy and link pie chart in **GSExpensesWorkbook.xlsx** to slide 6, size and center the pie chart on the slide. g. Close **GSExpensesWorkbook.xlsx..** Run presentation.	2	
14	Creating Footer	Create footer for handouts that prints title *2016 Sales Meeting*. Insert date in upper right corner.	2	
15-16	Printing, Saving	Print presentation as handout with six slides horizontally per page. Save and close **P-U2-A3-GSMtg.pptx**.	1	
17-19	Editing Excel	Open **GSExpensesWorkbook.xlsx**. Make changes as illustrated. Save, print, and close **GSExpensesWorkbook.xlsx**. Exit Excel	3	
20	Updating Links	With PowerPoint active, open **P-U2-A3-GSMtg.pptx**. Click Update Links button.	2	
21-22	Editing	With Slide 3 displayed, change data in embedded cells as illustrated. Run Presentation.	3	
23-24	Printing, Saving	Print handout with six slides horizontally per page. Save **P-U2-A3-GSMtg.pptx**.	1	
25	Formatting	Apply transition and sound of student's choosing.	2	
26-28	Setting Times	Use Rehearse Timings to set times for slides as illustrated. Set slide show to run continuously. Run presentation beginning with Slide 1. End show.	3	
29	Saving	Save and close **P-U2-A3-GSMtg.pptx**.	1	
		TOTAL POINTS	40	

Assessment 4: Apply Custom Animation Effects to a Travel Presentation
File: **P-U2-A4-NTAustralia.pptx**

Steps	Tasks	Criteria	Value	Score
1	Opening, Saving	Open **NTAustralia.pptx**. Save As **P-U2-A4-NTAustralia**.pptx	1	
2	Animation	With Slide 1 active, apply *Fly In* entrance animation effect to subtitle *Australia Tour*. Fly in from bottom.	2	

Steps	Tasks	Criteria	Value	Score
3	Slide Master	In Slide Master view, make the following changes: a. Click third slide master thumbnail. b. Apply a *Fly In* entrance animation effect to title. Fly in from top. c. Apply *Fly In* entrance animation effect to bulleted text. Fly in from left and dim to color of student's choosing when next bullet displays. d. Close Slide Master view.	5	
4	Freeform Motion	With Slide 5 active, select sun shape above *Sydney*. Change duration to *04.00*. Draw freeform motion path.	2	
5	Formatting	With Slide 6 active, make the following changes: a. Select bottom shape. b. Apply *Grow & Turn* entrance effect. c. Add Animation *Shrink & Turn* exit effect. d. Select middle shape and apply *Grow & Turn* entrance effect. e. Add Animation *Shrink & Turn* exit effect. f. Select top shape and apply *Grow & Turn* entrance effect. g. Stack shapes on top of each other hiding shapes behind.	5	
6	Saving	Save **P-U2-A4-NTAustralia.pptx**.	1	
7	Testing	With slide 1 active, run presentation, edit animation effects if necessary.	3	
8-9	Printing	Print handout with all slides printed horizontally on one page. Close **P-U2-A4-NTAustralia.pptx**.	1	
		TOTAL POINTS	20	

Assessment 5: Inspect a Presentation and Save a Presentation in Different Formats
File: **P-U2-A5-GreenDesignPres.pptx**

Steps	Tasks	Criteria	Value	Score
1	Opening, Saving	Open **P-U2-A1-GreenDesignPres.pptx**. Save As **P-U2-A5-GreenDesignPres**.	1	
2-5	Document Inspector, Compatibility Checker	Using Document Inspector, remove comments from presentation. Run compatibility checker. Save the presentation in PowerPoint 97-2003 format and name it **P-U2-A5-GreenDesignPres-2003format**. Close **P-U2-A5-GreenDesignPres-2003format.pptx**.	2	
6-9	Save as PDF	Open **P-U2-A5-GreenDesignPres.pptx**. Save As a PDF document. View presentation in Adobe Reader, Close Adobe Reader. Close **P-U2-A5-GreenSpacePres.pptx** without saving changes.	2	

Steps	Tasks	Criteria	Value	Score
10	Inserting Image	Capture an image of the Open dialog box and insert in a PowerPoint slide by completing the following steps: a. Display a new blank presentation with CTRL + N. b. Select *Blank* layout. c. Using File tab, click Open. d. Select *All Files (*.*)*. e. Scroll down the Open dialog box to display assessment files. f. Hold down Alt key and press the Print Screen button on keyboard. g. Click Cancel button to close Open dialog box. h. Click Paste button to insert image of Open dialog box into slide.	4	
11-12	Printing, Closing	Print full-page slide. Close presentation without saving.	1	
		TOTAL POINTS	10	

Writing Activities

Activity 1: Prepare and Format a Travel Presentation

File: **P-U2-Act1-NTVacations.pptx**

Steps	Tasks	Criteria	Value	Score
1	Opening, Printing Word	Open **NTVacations.docx** Word document. Print document.	1	
1	Creating Presentation	After reading document, create presentation highlighting main points of document. Proofread and correct errors.	10	
2	Timing	Rehearse and set times for slides. Student determines number of seconds for each slide.	2	
3	Inserting Song	With Slide 1 active, insert a song (search for *Summer*) from the Clip Art task pane. Change *Results should be* option to only *Audio*.	4	
4-5	Settings	Set presentation to run on endless loop. Play audio across all slides and continuously while presentation is running. Run presentation. End show.	4	
6	Saving, Printing	Save As **P-U2-Act1-NTVacations**. Print handouts with six slides horizontally per page. Close **P-U2-Act1-NTVacations.pptx**.	1	
		TOTAL POINTS	20	

Activity 2: Prepare and Format a Presentation on Media Files
File: **P-U1-Act2-AudioVideo.pptx**

Steps	Tasks	Criteria	Value	Score
1	Using Help	Use Help feature to learn more about audio and video file formats compatible with PowerPoint 2013. Search specifically for *audio and video file formats*.	2	
2	Creating Presentation	Based on reading information from Help, create presentation with *at least* the following specifications: Title Slide with title of presentation and student's name. At least two slides containing information on compatible audio file format including file format, extension, and brief description of format. At least two slides containing information on compatible video file format including file format, extension, and brief description of format. Optional: Connect to the Internet, search websites for downloading free audio clips. Include information on a slide with hyperlinks to the sites.	12	
3	Formatting	Format presentation appropriately. Add visual appeal to presentation.	5	
4	Saving, Printing	Save As **P-U2-Act2-AudioVideo**. Run presentation. Print handouts with six slides horizontally per page.	1	
		TOTAL POINTS	20	

Internet Research

Activity 1: Presenting Office 2013
File: **P-U2-Int-Office2013.pptx**

Steps	Tasks	Criteria	Value	Score
1	Exploring a Website	Connect to the Internet and explore the Microsoft website at **www.microsoft.com.** Browse the various categories and links. Learn how information is organized.	3	
2	Creating Presentation	Create presentation for someone who just purchased Office 2013 and wants to know how to find more information about the software from the Microsoft website. Include points or tips on where to find product release and information and technical support. Include hyperlinks to important pages at the Microsoft website. Present material in a clear, concise, and logical manner. Proofread and correct errors.	10	
3	Formatting	Add formatting and enhancements to presentation to make it as dynamic as possible.	6	
4	Saving, Printing, Closing	Save As **P-U2-Int-Office2013**. Run the presentation. Print handout with four slides per page. Close **P-U2-Int-Office2013. pptx**.	1	
		TOTAL POINTS	20	

Job Study

Creating a Skills Presentation

File: **P-U2-JobStudy.pptx**

Steps	Tasks	Criteria	Value	Score
1	Create a Presentation	Prepare a presentation to give at a local job fair. Open Word document **JobDescriptions.docx.** Print the document and then close.	3	
2	Creating Presentation	With the information in the document prepare slides that describe each job without using the starting salary. Use the Internet to locate two other jobs that interest you. Create a slide about the responsibilities of each job. Determine salary for the two jobs in search and use information to create a chart that displays the salary amount. Include the names in your presentation with hyperlinks. Save as **P-U2-JobStudy**. Run the presentation and then print as a handout with six slides printed horizontally per page. Save **P-U2-JobStudy.pptx.**	12	
		TOTAL POINTS:	15	

Benchmark PowerPoint 2013, Unit 1
Supplemental Assessments

Supplemental Assessment 1
Instructions

1. Create a PowerPoint presentation containing six slides with the following specifications:
   a. Apply the Banded design theme, the Blue II theme colors, and the Calibri-Cambria theme font.
   b. Create six slides that contain the text shown below:

   Slide 1 (Title Slide layout)

   Title = Worldwide Enterprises

   Subtitle = (delete the subtitle placeholder)

   Slide 2 (Section Header layout)

   Title = Distribution Department

   Subtitle = Planning Meeting

   Slide 3 (Title and Content layout)

   Market

   - Market share
   - Current market
   - Future market
   - Market indicators
   - Consumer profile

   Slide 4 (Title and Content layout)

   Competition

   - Current competition
   - Emerging competition
   - Competitors' strengths
   - Competitors' weaknesses
   - Pricing

   Slide 5 (Title and Content layout)

   Product Fulfillment

   - Distribution
     o Costs
     o Reliability
     o System needs

- Packaging
  - o Pricing
  - o Appearance
  - o Strengths/weaknesses
  - Slide 6 (Title Only layout)
    - Title = European Division
1. Insert, format, and size a clip art image of your choosing in Slide 3 that refers to *Marketing*.
2. Insert, format, and size a clip art image of your choosing in Slide 5 that refers to *Business*.
3. Insert a shape of your choosing in Slide 6 and then insert the following text inside the shape:

   London Department

   Nicholas Severson, Director

   Paris Department

   Claudine Limeaux, Director

   Berlin Department

   Henry Schueller, Director

4. Apply any additional formatting to enhance the appearance of each slide.
5. Create a footer containing your name and apply it to all slides.
6. Save the completed presentation and name it **P-U1-SA1**.
7. Print the presentation as a handout with all six slides printed horizontally on the same page.
8. Close **P-U1-SA1.pptx**.

Note that the following are suggested rubrics. Instructors should feel free to customize the rubrics to suit your grading standards and/or to adjust the point values.

Suggested Scoring Distribution: Above average: student completes 80% or more of task(s); average = student completes 70-79% of task(s); below average = student completes 69% or less of task(s)

Rubric
Supplemental Assessment 1
File: **P-U1-SA1.pptx**

Steps	Tasks	Criteria	Value	Score
1a	**Feature**	Apply Banded design theme, Blue II theme colors, and Calibri-Cambria theme font	**3**	
1b	**Typing/Accuracy**	Type content of six slides Check spelling	**3**	

Steps	Tasks	Criteria	Value	Score
1b	**Feature**	Apply proper layout Slide 1 – Title Slide 2 – Section Header Slides 3-5 – Title and Content Slide 6 – Title Only	4	
2,3	**Feature/Editing**	Slides 3 & 5 – Clip art Appropriate clip art inserted, resized, and positioned	4	
4	**Feature/Editing**	Slide 6 – Insert shape and insert text within shape	4	
5	**Finishing**	Format slides Run though slides and check for layout, color choices, etc.	3	
6	**Editing**	Insert footer containing name on all slides	2	
7,8	**Accuracy/ Finishing**	Print as a handout with six slides horizontally on the same page Save	2	
		TOTAL POINTS	25	

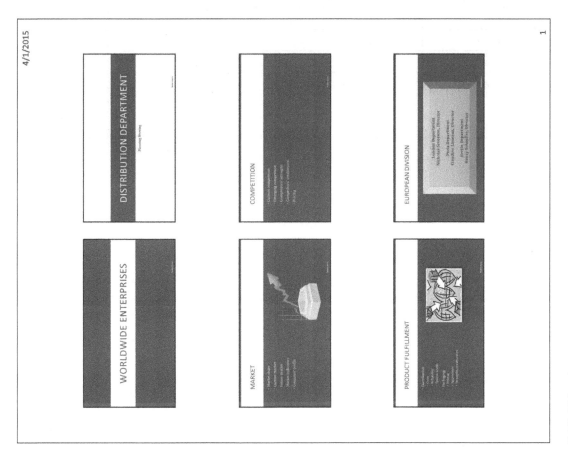

Supplemental Assessment 2

Instructions

1. Open **P-U1-SA.pptx** and save it as **P-U1-SA2**.
2. Apply the Style 11 background style.
3. On Slide 4, apply WordArt to the title *Competition* and format the WordArt to enhance the appearance of the slide.
4. Apply the *Split* transition, change the duration to *00.75*, and then apply to all slides.
5. Have the slides advance automatically after 00:05:00 seconds. Remove the *On Mouse Click* option, and apply the changes to all slides.
6. Save the presentation and print it as a handout with all six slides printed horizontally on the same page.
7. Close **P-U1-SA2.pptx**.

Rubric

Supplemental Assessment 2

File: **P-U1-SA2.pptx**

Steps	Tasks	Criteria	Value	Score
1	**Organization**	Open presentation, use Save As	1	
2	**Feature**	Style 11 background style	2	
3	**Editing**	Slide 4 Word Art	2	
4	**Feature**	*Split* transition on all slides, with duration set to *00:75*	2	
5	**Feature**	Slides advance automatically after 5 seconds Remove the *On Mouse Click* option Apply to all	3	
		TOTAL POINTS	10	

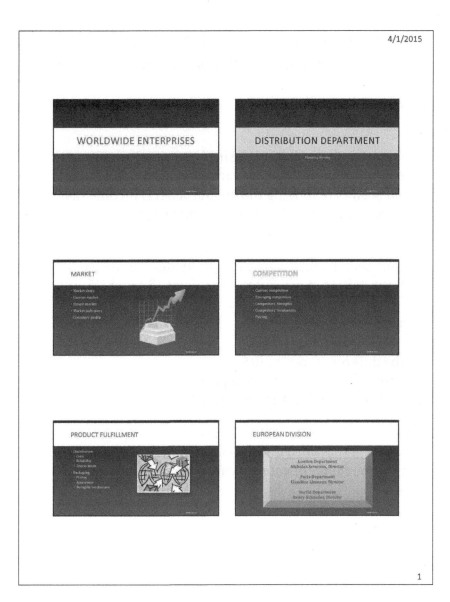

P-U1-SA2.pptx

Benchmark PowerPoint 2013, Unit 2
Supplemental Assessments

Supplemental Assessment 1

Instructions

You own your own software consulting business working as a freelance trainer. You have become interested in investing for your retirement. You are very conservative with your money and are looking to cut your federal income taxes. One of your friends suggests that you check out Individual Retirement Accounts (IRAs).

Part 1

Using more than one search engine, research Individual Retirement Accounts (IRAs) on the Internet. Be certain to check out the site www.IRA.com. You are particularly interested in the following questions:

- What is an IRA?
- How does an IRA work?
- What are the different types of IRAs?
- What has been the performance of a particular IRA?
- Where to find additional IRA information?

Part 2

Using the information in the Word document **P-U2-SA1-IRAs-FAQs-DataFile.docx** and the information you found in your research, prepare an informational presentation explaining IRAs.

1. Design your presentation to include:
   a. 10 to 15 slides
   b. Choose a design and modify the slide master design to include an appropriate clip art image
   c. Transitions on all slides
   d. Clip art images
   e. On the first slide, include WordArt, your name, course, and date
   f. At least one shape
   g. Slide numbers and your name in the footer on all slides except the title slide
2. You may copy text from the Word document to a slide or import text as suits your needs. There is more information in the document than is needed.
3. Include a chart prepared from the Excel worksheet **P-U2-SA1-IRAs-PastQuarterlyReturns-DataFile.xlsx**.
4. Include the following features:
   a. On the *Where to find additional IRA information?* slide include a hyperlink to www.IRA.com and your choice of two other websites.
   b. To answer the question *What are the different types of IRAs?* do the following:
      i. Create a summary slide that lists the five different types of IRAs
      ii. Create a separate slide for each type of IRA that gives details about that specific IRA

      i. On the summary slide (the slide created in 4bi), create a hyperlink from each specific type of IRA to the individual detailed slide (the slides you created in 4bii)

     ii. On each of the detailed slides (the slides you created in 4bii), create an action button that links back to the summary slide (the slide created in 4bi)

1. Save your presentation as **P-U2-SA1-IRAInfo**. Print the slides as a handout with six slides printed horizontally per page.

Note that the following are suggested rubrics. Instructors should feel free to customize the rubrics to suit your grading standards and/or to adjust the point values.

Rubric
Supplemental Assessment 1

File: **P-U2-SA1-IRAInfo.pptx**

Steps	Tasks	Criteria	Value	Score
1a,2	Organization	10 to 15 slides Summarized material Proper amount of material on a page Material presented in an organized fashion	10	
1b	Feature	Choose appropriate design and modify Slide Master to include clip art	5	
1c	Feature	Transitions on all slides	4	
1d	Feature/Editing	Appropriate clip art and/or images inserted, resized and positioned	3	
1e	Feature/Editing	WordArt on opening screen	3	
1f	Feature/Editing	One shape	3	
1g	Feature	Footer with page numbers and student name on all slides but the title slide	3	
3	Feature	Chart from Excel data file	3	
4a	Features	Hyperlinks to www.IRA.com and two other websites	3	
4b	Feature	Links from the summary slide *What are the different types of IRAs?* to slide containing each individual type	5	
4b	Feature	Links from each type back to the summary page	5	
5	Accuracy/ Finishing	Print as a handout with six slides on the same page Save	3	
		TOTAL POINTS	50	

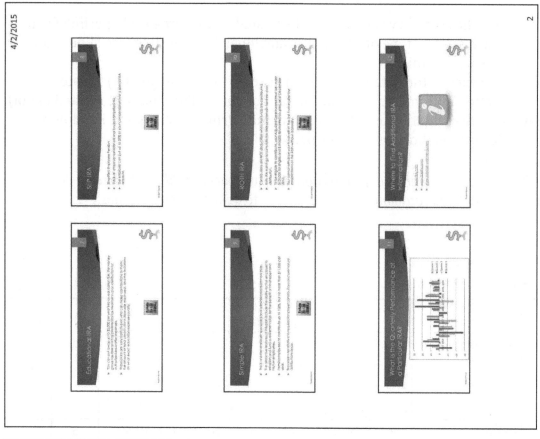

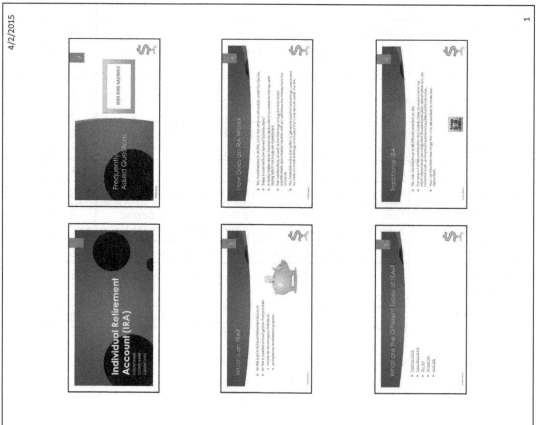

Benchmark PowerPoint 2013 Supplemental Skills Assessments

Supplemental Assessment 2

Instructions

You are pleased with the presentation that you created for Supplemental Assessment 1. However, you would like your composition consultant, Helene Herlitz, and your Certified Financial Planner, Suzanne Parchetta, to review your presentation. As the saying goes, it is always good to get a second opinion. Save the presentation completed in Supplemental Assessment 1 as **P-U2-SA2-IRAInfo**.

Part 1

You will prepare the presentation for review. Before you do, add the following changes:

1. Provide custom animation on at least three slides.
2. On the *What are the different types of IRAs?* summary slide, use a SmartArt graphic with text instead of just text to represent the different types of IRAs on the slide. Reestablish any hyperlinks that were broken.
3. Add three comments to your presentation, such as, "Do you think this text should be condensed?"
4. Insert appropriate presentation properties.

Part 2

1. Helene and Suzanne, after careful review of the presentation, have suggested that you add a second chart showing the performance of an additional IRA. Using the resources available to you on the Internet, select a second IRA and chart its performance for a comparable amount of time as you used to answer the question *What has been the performance of a particular IRA?* using PowerPoint's chart feature. Save the presentation.
2. When you are satisfied that your presentation is in its final form, save it as a PowerPoint show.
3. Submit all electronic copies of files and folders to your instructor, along with a printout of the show as a handout with six slides printed horizontally per page.

Rubric

Supplemental Assessment 2

Files: **P-U2-SA2-IRAInfo.pptx**

  P-U2-SA2-IRAInfo.ppsx

Steps	Tasks	Criteria	Value	Score
	Organization	Open presentation, use Save As	**2**	
Part 1 1	**Feature**	Custom animation on at least three slides	**6**	
2	**Feature/Editing**	SmartArt graphic with text as hyperlink	**8**	
		Check that hyperlinks work		
3	**Feature**	Three comments	**3**	

Steps	Tasks	Criteria	Value	Score
4	**Feature**	Presentation properties	3	
Part 2 1	**Editing**	Insert a chart found on the Internet using the chart feature	10	
2	**Feature**	Save presentation as a PowerPoint show	3	
		TOTAL POINTS	35	

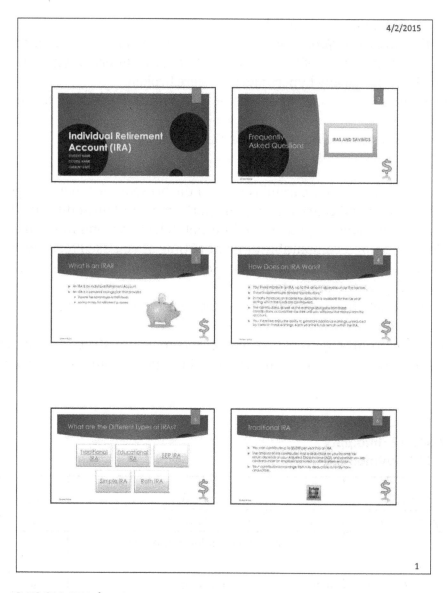

P-U2-SA2-IRAInfo.pptx

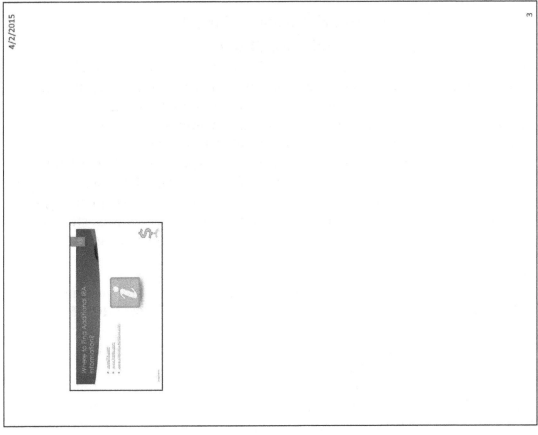

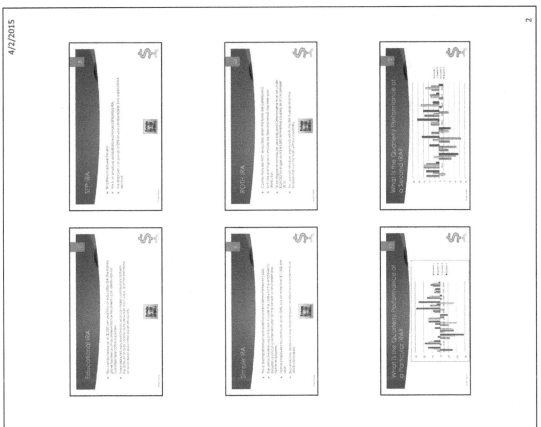

Benchmark PowerPoint 2013
Final Case Study

Scenario: You are on a temporary work assignment at Lambton Logistics located in New Orleans. Lambton Logistics provides administrative services to various companies. Your expertise in PowerPoint has been requested to assist management in creating a presentation on planning and organizing meetings. As you work through each activity, additional information will be provided as needed.

This case study will allow you to exercise creativity and polish your PowerPoint skills. In each activity, specific step-by-step instructions may not be provided to simulate a more realistic workplace assignment. Some instructions may appear vague or not comprehensive, but they are purposefully open-ended to allow each student to do original work and showcase individual creativity in problem solving.

Part 1

1. Download an appropriate template from the Internet related to meetings.
2. Import the presentation from the Word document **P-FCS-PlanandOrgMtngs-DataFile.docx**.
3. Make the first slide *Planning and Organizing Meetings* and apply an appropriate layout. Add your name, college or institution, and date.
4. Apply transitions on all slides.
5. Input your name and the page number as a footer on all but the first slide.
6. Adjust the Slide Master so your name appears along the left margin of the page. (You may need to adjust other footer elements so text does not overlap.)

Part 2

1. Insert a new Title Only slide after Slide 5 and insert the slide title and SmartArt graphic shown on the next page. (Your slide design may vary.) Apply formatting to enhance the appearance of the graphic and then apply animation so that each point comes in one by one.
   a. Issue
   b. Agenda (Brings issue before the group)
   c. Meeting (Discuss the issue)
   d. Minutes (Report the group's discussion/decision)
   e. Issue (Completely dealt with)
2. Add the bottom arrow shape (*U-Turn Arrow*) plus the word *or* to the SmartArt graphic. Apply an entrance animation to the arrow and then the word *or* to display after 7e from above.

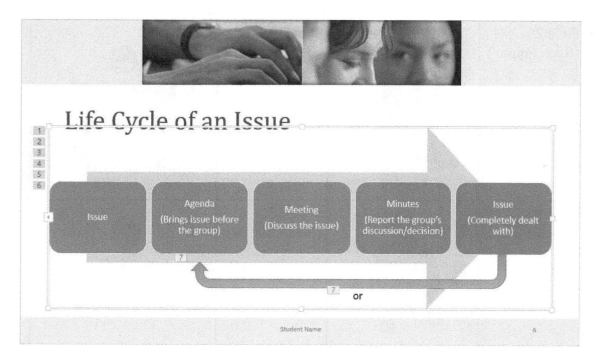

Part 3

1. Add clip art images to at least three slides.
2. On Slide 10 (*Determining Number of Attendees*):
   a. Change the color of the word *synergy* so that it stands out.
   b. Add a text box that brings in the definition of synergy (shown below) when the mouse is clicked. Change the text to be the same color chosen for *synergy*.
      iii. *Ideas and products of a group of people developed through interaction with each other*
3. On Slide 4 (*Organizing Meetings*):
   a. Fade the bulleted text so that it disappears off the screen when clicked.
   b. Add a text box that appears automatically after the text has disappeared. The text box should contain the text shown on the next page. Format the text so that it stands out.
      iii. Everyone from organizer to participant has a role to play in ensuring successful meetings.
4. Add the following diagrams to the slides as indicated using shapes. Position, size, and color the diagrams to enhance the visual appearance.

Slide 25 (Rectangular)		Slide 27 (U-shaped)	
Slide 26 (Circular)		Slide 27 (Semicircular)	

1. Using the bulleted list of the four different types of seating arrangements, create hyperlinks in Slide 24 to the slides containing the correlating seating arrangements found in Slides 25, 26, and 27.
2. Insert action buttons in the presentation. Make sure to create an action button that will return the presentation to the first slide.
3. Add any other animation to enhance the presentation.
4. Save the presentation as **P-FCS.pptx**.

Part 4

1. Insert appropriate presentation properties.
2. On the last slide, delete the last bullet: *What should I discuss with my supervisor? What can I do on my own?* Save the presentation.
3. Print the presentation as a handout with six slides printed horizontally per page.
4. You have decided that you would like to make adjustments to the handout, so you decide to use Word for the handouts. Make the handouts with blank lines next to the slides. Link the presentation. Bold the text in the first column. Save the document as **P-FCS-Handouts.docx**.
5. This presentation is being given at the various Lambton Logistics locations. You are not sure if all locations have PowerPoint. Save the presentation so that it may be given at any location, using the name **P-FCS2**.
6. Submit all electronic copies of files and folders to your instructor, along with any printouts.

Benchmark PowerPoint 2013
Final Case Study Rubric

Final Case Study

Files: **P-FCS.pptx**

P-FCS-Handout.docx

P-FCS2.ppsx

Steps	Tasks	Criteria	Value	Score
Part 1 **1**	**Feature**	Download template from Internet (student choice) and apply	**5**	
2,3	**Organization/ Edit**	Import presentation from Word Delete first blank slide (if necessary) Add name, college or institution, and date to first slide First slide should be a title slide (title layout)	**6**	
4	**Feature**	Transitions on all slides	**3**	
5	**Feature/Edit**	Name and page number on all but first	**3**	
6	**Feature/Edit**	Slide Master – name at left margin	**3**	
Part 2 **1**	**Feature/Edit**	New Slide 6 – SmartArt	**5**	
1,2	**Feature**	Slide 6 – SmartArt animation	**5**	
2	**Feature**	Slide 6 – shape and text box added below SmartArt with animation applied	**5**	
Part 3 **1**	**Feature/Edit**	At least three clip art images added effectively throughout the presentation	**3**	
2a	**Feature/Edit**	Slide 10 – synergy – stands out – color	**3**	
2b	**Feature/Edit**	Definition – added with animation	**3**	
3	**Feature**	Slide 4 – Fade text when clicked New text box appears – after previous disappears Text stands out	**5**	
4	**Feature/Edit**	Diagrams using shapes to Slides 25, 26, and 27	**8**	
5	**Feature**	Hyperlinks on Slides 24 linked to Slides 25, 26, and 27	**4**	
6	**Feature**	Insert action buttons on all slides Last slide – action button to return presentation to first slide	**5**	
6	**Feature**	Other animation to enhance presentation	**5**	

Steps	Tasks	Criteria	Value	Score
Part 4 **1**	**Feature**	Presentation properties	**3**	
2	**Feature**	Delete text – check last slide – *What should I discuss with my supervisor? What can I do on my own?* should not be there.	**1**	
3	**Finishing**	Print handouts – 6 per page horizontally	**3**	
4	**Finishing**	Export to Word as handout; link; lines next to slides Bold first column	**4**	
5	**Finishing**	Save presentation as a show – .ppsx	**3**	
		TOTAL POINTS	**85**	

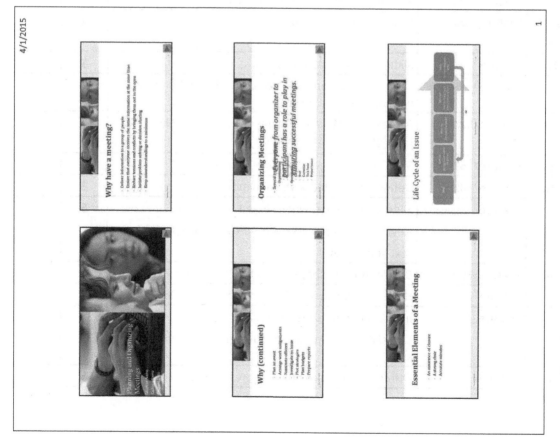

4/1/2015

P-FCS.pptx (1 of 5)

1

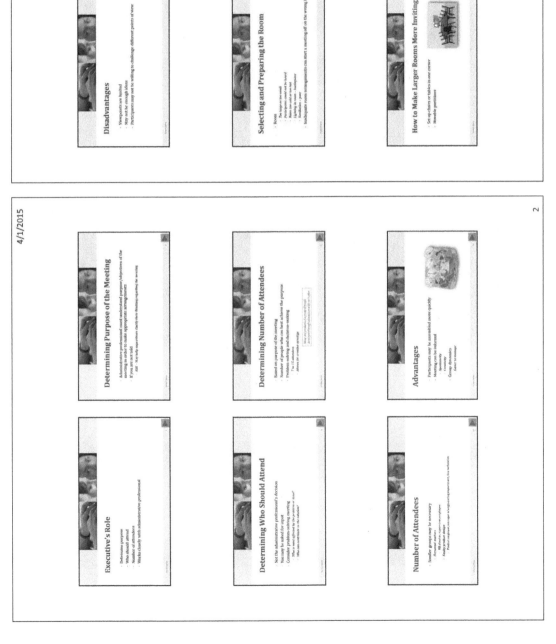

P-FCS.pptx (3 of 5)

P-FCS.pptx (2 of 5)

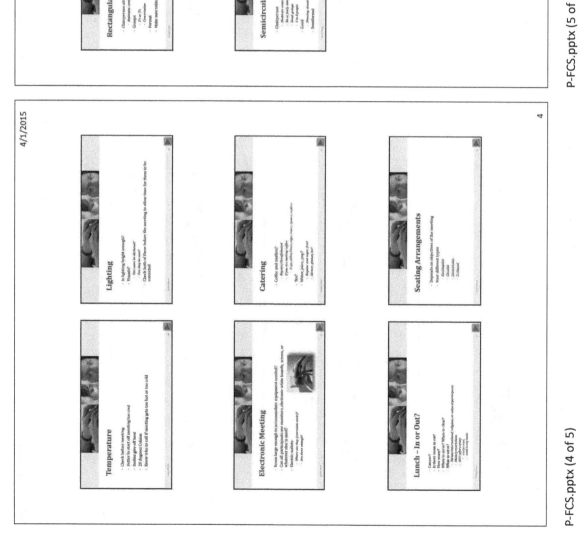

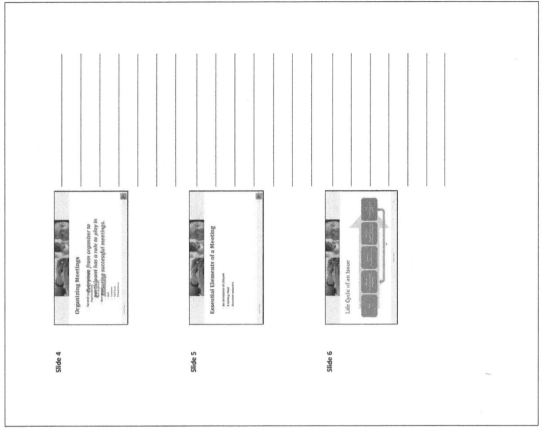

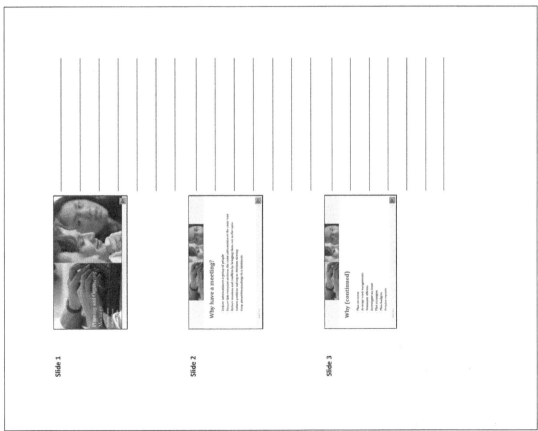

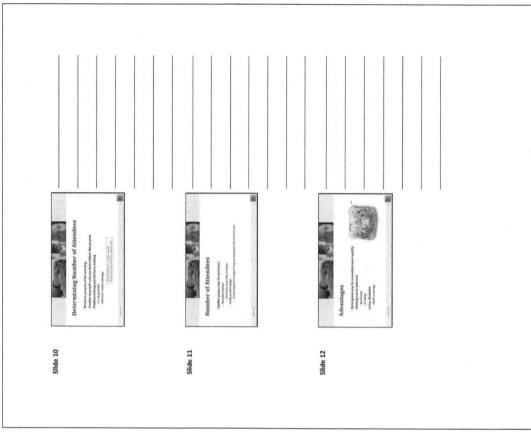

Slide 10

Slide 11

Slide 12

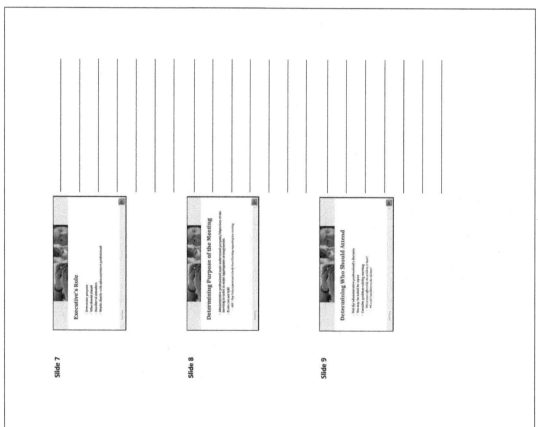

Slide 7

Slide 8

Slide 9

Benchmark PowerPoint 2013 Final Case Studies

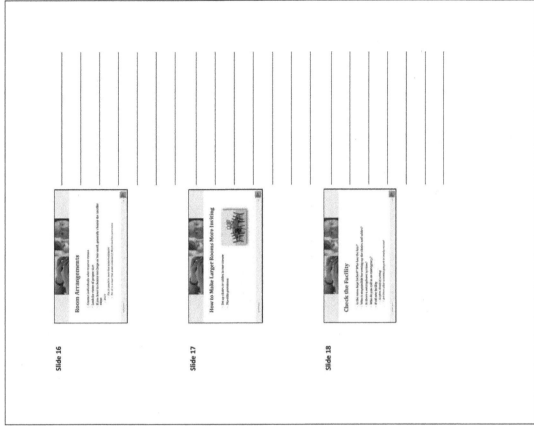

Slide 16 — Room Arrangements

Slide 17 — How to Make Larger Rooms More Inviting

Slide 18 — Check the Facility

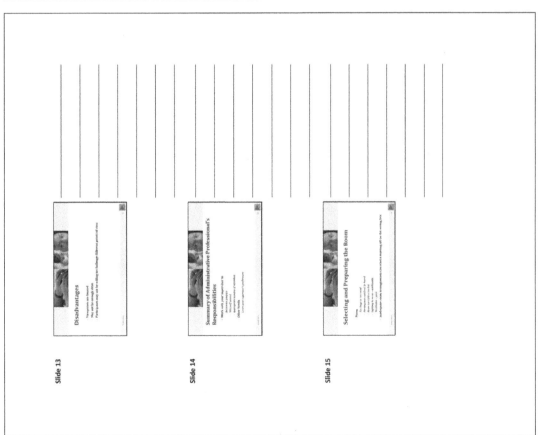

Slide 13 — Disadvantages

Slide 14 — Summary of Administrative Professional's Responsibilities

Slide 15 — Selecting and Preparing the Room

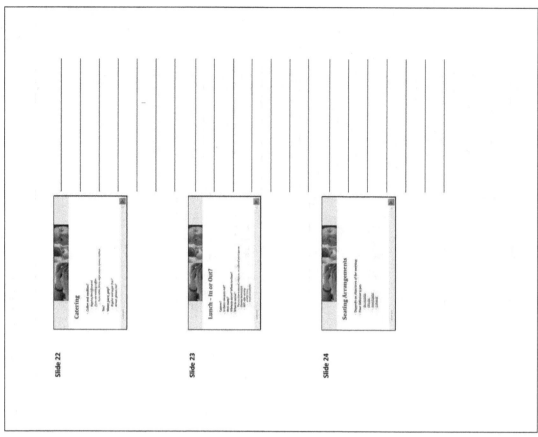

Slide 22

Slide 23

Slide 24

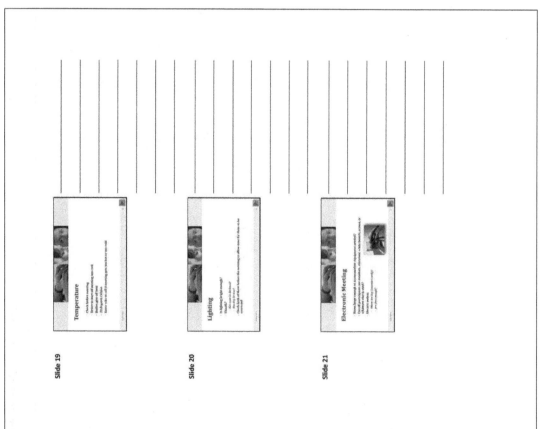

Slide 19

Slide 20

Slide 21

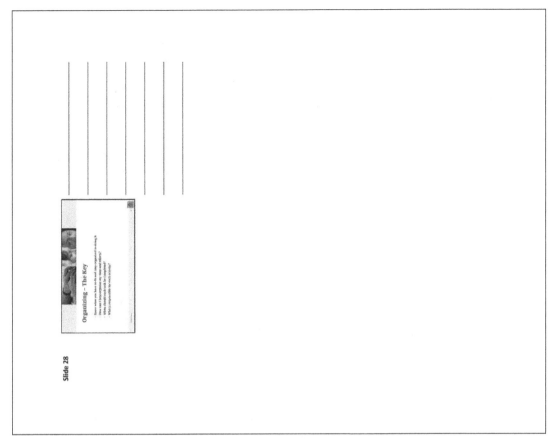

Slide 28

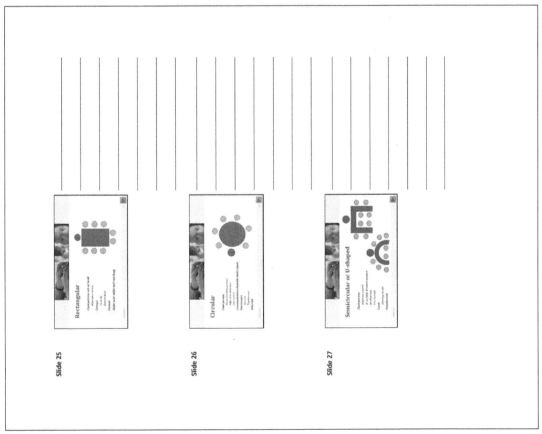

Slide 25

Slide 26

Slide 27